AUTO-EROTICISM

When this work was first published in the first half of the last century, sexology and the unprejudiced study of sexual activity was in its infancy. In his study of human sexual behaviour, Kinsey was able to state that the majority of human beings had masturbated at one time or another but to us today this seems quite an astonishing statement to have had to make.

The study of human sexuality was surrounded by ignorance and superstition, and the medical profession was regretably the worst offender and the most ignored. In such a climate, Dr. Stekel's book was a revelation much ahead of its time.

AUTO-EROTICISM

A Psychiatric Study of Onanism and Neurosis

Wilhelm Stekel

Routledge
Taylor & Francis Group

LONDON AND NEW YORK

Published 2014 by Routledge
First published in 2004 by
Kegan Paul International

This edition first published in 2011 by
Routledge
2 Park Square, Milton Park, Abingdon, Oxfordshire OX14 4RN

Simultaneously published in the USA and Canada
by Routledge
711 Third Avenue, New York, NY 10017

First issued in paperback 2014

Routledge is an imprint of the Taylor & Francis Group, an informa business

British Library Cataloguing in Publication Data
A catalogue record for this book is available from the British Library

ISBN 978-0-710-30894-8 (hbk)
ISBN 978-1-138-87988-1 (pbk)

Publisher's Note
The publisher has gone to great lengths to ensure the quality of this reprint
but points out that some imperfections in the original copies may be
apparent. The publisher has made every effort to contact original copyright
holders and would welcome correspondence from those they have been
unable to trace.

CONTENTS

FOREWORD

by

EMIL A. GUTHEIL, M.D.

We usually take medical progress for granted and are inclined to forget that at the beginning of each advance stands an individual, an independent thinker and intuitive observer who dares to disagree with the existing views and to expose himself to the animosity of his conservative contemporaries.

Today we consider the aseptic management of obstetrical deliveries as self-evident and we tend to forget that there was a time when an individual, Semmelweiss, working at an obstetric clinic in Vienna, dared to challenge his profession with the bold pronouncement that it was the physician himself who with his unsterile hands was carrying the puerperal infection and death to the women in childbirth. Ridiculed and ostracized at first, Semmelweiss later was rightly referred to as the "Savior of Mothers."

Conditions in the field of sexology were also controlled by ignorance. Today, when Kinsey in his study is able to state that the majority of human beings have masturbated at one time or another; when the problem of auto-erotism represents a topic of frank discussions in study groups

1

and mental hygiene classes of colleges, we do not
bother to acknowledge the fact that many years
before Kinsey, Freud proved the pansexualism of
the child, and Stekel came out with his epoch-
making clinical observations regarding masturbation.   Stekel maintained that if it were true that
masturbation was as harmful as the contemporary
medical world believed, the majority of human
beings in this world would be found in hospitals
and insane asylums.

What at first caused the pioneering Stekel to
suffer a great deal of opposition from and distrust
by his colleagues was his claim that, in sexual matters, doctors were dangerous laymen!   Dangerous,
because they gave professional advice to their
trusting patients; laymen, because in sexual matters they were not free from superstitions and
prejudices to which they themselves had been exposed when they were young.   Stekel's ingenious
observations which constitute the contents of the
present work have dealt a deadly blow to these
superstitions.   By submitting this work to the
scrutiny of the medical profession, Stekel helped
to free the young generation from the all-pervad-
ing feeling of anxiety, the hypochondriacal antici-
pation, and the profound guilt feelings caused by
misinformation.   For this accomplishment alone,
the great psychotherapist deserves the name "Savior of Youth."

According to Stekel there are two types of
masturbation.   One is physiological; the other is

pathological. The first, according to Freud, represents a stage in the psychosexual development of the individual. It is a passing phenomenon, an activity which as a rule is given up in the course of time. It is sublimated by physical and mental diversions, and is ultimately replaced by the heterosexual adjustment. This type of masturbation is harmless and does not need medical attention.

The pathological form of masturbation is one that carries a stigma of compulsiveness, and it is practiced although opportunities for heterosexual adjustment are available. These opportunities are eschewed in favor of auto-erotic activity. Such a behavior bespeaks a neurotic rift in the patient's personality, a deviation of his sexual interest, the existence of manifest or latent paraphilia. It is the smoke that indicates the presence of a fire, that is, it represents a symptom of a disease. The disease itself requires full medical attention.

In the current book, Stekel treats the delicate problem with tact and detachment. The publishers are to be commended for their decision to acquaint the English speaking public with one of the pioneering works of psychiatric literature. This edition will also terminate the repeated acts of intellectual piracy and make it possible that Stekel's spiritual property, particularly his original ideas concerning auto-erotism, will no longer be presented as the proud discovery of other medical and non-medical authors.

Grateful humanity sets monuments to the great

liberators of mankind, to the men who bring freedom to the oppressed. But the greatest liberators are those who free suffering mankind from its own ignorance.

New York City, September, 1949.

INTRODUCTION

PROBLEMS OF AUTO-EROTISM

by

Fredric Wertham, M.D.

Our social attitude towards sex is strange rather than constructive. Semi-pornographic comic books are offered to minors by the thousands, and the sale of these sex stimuli to children is upheld by would-be defenders of free speech. At the same time, a scientific book giving a scientific clinical presentation of so important a subject as auto-erotism needs an introduction, if not an apology.

It is not difficult to recommend Dr. Stekel's book on auto-erotism, for apart from it there is no modern scientific book or monograph on the subject that would fulfill scientific standards. The sparsity of good literature on auto-erotism is an important phenomenon in psychology and sociology. This is the more so since publications on the subject are so controversial and range all the way to the misinforming, the misleading, and the outright superstitious. I am referring not only to popular literature, but also to official literature giving instructions to young people and to scientific literature, itself.

Popular literature is usually not based on clinical and psychiatric studies at all. Although denying that it does so, it frequently scares people in a manner far more detrimental to mental health than is generally acknowledged. One outstanding feature of popular writing on the subject is that if it is written on a medical level it stresses the harmful moral effects; if written on a religious or moral basis, it stresses the harmful medical effects (which are fancied to exist, but of which the writer has no scientific knowledge).

Some material given to young people by official agencies, far from being helpful, is injurious to mental health. For example, a pamphlet addressed to boys and issued by the U. S. Public Health Service says auto-erotism (which it terms "self-abuse") "may seriously hinder a boy's progress towards vigorous manhood." What better method is there to instill a deep hypochondriasis, loss of self-respect, and severe inferiority feelings in an adolescent? And it is, of course, this kind of misinformation which at certain times may cause such tension states of guilt and shame that the young boy may be driven to the very act he, himself, wants to avoid.

Scientific references to auto-erotism are characterized to a large extent not by frank facing of clinical questions, but by ambiguity and absence of well-documented scientific judgment of concrete data. Unable to free themselves from traditional views of harmful physical and mental effects, authors go in for all sorts of evasions. Maybe, they say, the effects are not so bad as used to be thought,—but then they go on to paint fanciful pictures of harm that may be done if the auto-erotism becomes a "habit"; if it starts too early,— or too late; if it lasts too long or is done by the wrong method; if it is excessive; if it is practiced by a child—or by an adult, by a person who is married (or who isn't); if it is practiced "automatically" or is accompanied by fantasies.

It is interesting how little work has been done on this subject and how many speculations and generalizations have been built on an emotional rather than a scientific basis. A few examples from medical literature will give a picture of this confusion. A medical treatise, "A Study of Masturbation and the Psychosexual Life," which appeared in two editions, states that masturbation is not abnormal in young children, but is always abnormal in adults. It gives this definition: "As ordinarily practiced, masturbation is an act to produce a pure form of sensory pleasure bought at the expense of high moral tone."

"A Practical Treatise on Disorders of the Sexual Function in the Male and Female" designates auto-erotism specifically as a "disease." This book gives pernicious advice to physicians with regard to the detection of this "disease" in young boys. The author states: "The physician should not neglect an examination of the genitals in any suspicious case, and very often the local symptoms will tell the tale.   In young boys, after an examination of the genitals by the physician, whether he finds anything there or not, it is often advisable for the physician, if he is reasonably sure of his ground from the general symptoms, to tell the boy immediately after the examination that he masturbates.   The boy, being taken off his guard, if guilty, will imagine that the physician can tell by the examination, and will often admit the truth at once."   No surer method can be devised for starting a chronic hypochondriacal reaction in an adolescent—or in a grown-up, for that matter, than to give him the false impression, the hocus-pocus of the medicine man, that he has injured himself to such an extent that a physician can detect it at sight.   The results of such methods can never be helpful and are always harmful.   And yet they are frequently employed and I know of cases where they have been the precipitating cause of suicidal attempts.

Unfortunately, even neuropsychiatrists who are highly authoritative in other fields lapse in this one.   A famous neurologist, and one-time president of the New York Academy of Medicine had this to say in a symposium on "The Prevention of Nervous and Mental Disorders": "Any man with even half the experience I have had in neurological and psychiatric practice cannot doubt the evils of masturbation.   Occasionally masturbation does no harm, but where it becomes a habit it affects the entire individual; it changes him; it taxes him emotionally, his powers, his energy as a working individual; and it wrecks him when carried to excess. I consider it one of the most harmful practices, and when you tell me that 99% of men masturbate, I do not believe it. They may make an occasional attempt in early life, but I should be sorry for our manhood if they were all masturbators; I am sure they are not and never were, not all of them at any rate. I have the greatest admiration for Freud, but he is not the only psychologist that ever lived."

In a recent encyclopedia, this anachronism occurs: "The fact is well recognized that excessive masturbation leads to moodiness, periods of depression and a chain of symptoms closely resembling neurasthenia."

The average practitioner is apt to underrate the amount of human misery caused by false information about auto-erotism handed on from generation to generation. Here Dr. Stekel has performed a pioneer task in mental hygiene.

Wherever the question of auto-erotism comes up as a complaint, the physician faces a delicate task of psychotherapy. He can, and often does, make serious errors. He should not laugh off the superstitious results which a patient imagines he suffers from. For he thereby prevents his patient from telling him other fears and anxieties. On the whole, the physician has to guard against two extreme attitudes in connection with this subject.

One such attitude is to be absolutely permissive and tell the patient to do whatever he likes, there is nothing wrong whatsoever. Man is not a machine. His fears exist in a setting of self-imposed moral rules and regulations. His anxieties do not come only from fears of physical harm, but from fear of moral harm, too. It should be obvious that the physician cannot disregard the personality of the patient who worries.

The other extreme is to make a mountain out of something that certainly does not deserve to be so magnified. I have known instances where, in ordinary cases of worries about auto-erotism, even prolonged psychoanalytic treatment was advised. In this way a natural concern about sexual development was turned by the psychiatrist or psychoanalyst into a neurotic preoccupation.

In most cases where adults take notice of auto-erotism in children, the question is insignificant from the point of view of the child's objective mental and physical health. But nothing is insignificant which is connected with so much guilt feeling, fear and worry on the part of the child and/or the parent. There is a large middleground where individual problems of auto-erotism should be taken up sensibly, frankly, and seriously—but not too seriously. And for this Dr. Stekel's book has been a great help.

Es gibt Bücher, welche für die Seele und Gesundheit einen umgekehrten Wert haben, je nachdem die niedere Seele, die niedrigere Lebenskraft oder aber die höhere und gewaltigere sich ihrer bedienen.

NIETZSCHE

I

The Sexuality of the Child—Coitus During Childhood—Why Physicians have overlooked the Sexuality of Children—The Asexualization and Idealization of the Child—Account of Infantile Onanism—Two Types of the Practice—Masturbating Children Regarded as Epileptic—Freud's Views Regarding Infantile Onanism—The so-called Latent Period—Prevalence of the Habit among the Talented and among the Neurotic Children—Paraphilia, Parapathy, and Paralogy—New Names for New Viewpoints—Discredited Views Regarding Masturbation—The Question of a Definition—The Various Forms of the Habit—Various Statistical Data on the Frequency of the Habit—Everybody is addicted to the Habit—Neurosis is a Consequence of Abstinence, not the Result of the Habit—Does Masturbation lead to Neurasthenia?—Analysis of a Case of so-called Neurasthenia—Analysis of Person fond of Children who protects himself against Crime through Masturbation—A Masturbating Asocial Personality—Masturbation as Social Protection against Sexual Crimes.

AUTO-EROTISM

I

Some books have a reverse influence on mind and health, depending on whether they reach the lower mind, the lower vital resources, or whether they are utilized by the higher and the more powerful inner forces.

NIETZSCHE

Our sexual life begins with the day of our birth and it ends with death. Other investigators go further and ascribe even to the fœtus a certain degree of sexuality. That is something I am not disposed to deny but it is a view I cannot corroborate. On the other hand I know through my personal observations, extending over many years, that heretofore we have been wrongly instructed regarding the beginnings of sexuality. It has been always held that in the normal human being sexuality awakens first with puberty. Whenever this happened earlier, the occurrence was regarded as something exceptional and as a sign of a psychopathic

constitution.   I should have to fill volumes if I
endeavored to quote all the modern authorities that
are still of this opinion.   It has always surprised me
to find that physicians know so little about the
sexual life of children, notwithstanding their opportunities for thorough observation besides the memories of their own early youth.   I was formerly unacquainted with "spiritual scotoma," or the will-not-
to-see.   The sexual sphere contains too much that is
intimately personal so that not all physicians are
able to approach it with an unprejudiced attitude.
Thus it comes about that ridiculous prejudices have
been maintained for centuries as scientific truths;
and that is why, in sexual matters, to this day
unprejudiced lay persons and experienced prostitutes are capable of properly instructing many a
young disciple of Æsculapius.

How is it possible that all persons,—mothers,
fathers, physicians, nurses,—should overlook the
child's early sexual excitations?   It is utterly impossible to dismiss this fact as a mere chance occurrence.   It is a social phenomenon, and it stands out
perhaps as the most significant indication of civilized
man's attitude towards sexuality.   For the phenomenon reveals an unwillingness-to-see.   It is not an
oversight,—it is a *Vorübersehen,* a deliberate refusal
to see.

At this juncture I want to trace out a fundamental difference between my account of the dis-

orders of the sexual functions and the previous views. Formerly the account of these disorders was purely descriptive, or individual. On my part I endeavor to examine these disorders from their aspect as social manifestations and at every step to trace the relations of the individual to the social group. The oversight of the sexuality of childhood is also a significant social manifestation which discloses that humanity is struggling against sexuality. This deliberate oversight necessarily involves also the medical profession. Physicians are not immune against social determinism any more than any other group. That is the reason why the most famous investigators of sexual problems have heretofore ignored certain facts.[1]

Naturally when *Freud* revealed anew the sexuality of children, he encountered most bitter opposition. The will-not-to-see has partly enshrouded also the one investigator who has described over again the phenomenon which was always clear and obvious for any one to perceive who cared to see. That *Freud* was able to see it may be due partly to the fact that we live in an age characterized by a strong reaction against the old policy of covering up sexual matters. For, independently of *Freud,* many investigators began to disclose sexual facts. The time was ripe for

---

[1] *Moll* regards as pathological the manifestations of the sexual instinct before the 7th year. Were that so the world would consist entirely of morbid individuals and sexuality itself would have to be regarded as a morbidity.

light. In fact, I was the first—independently of
Freud's teachings—to point out, as far back as
1895, the prevalence of coitus among children.

What I then remarked seems to me so relevant that
I reproduce below the significant parts of the earlier
contribution:

That coitus during early childhood is an occurrence far from rare is a fact which appears to be
but little known in medical circles. Some of the
local specialists whom I have interrogated told me
they had no information on the subject, and met my
remarks relating thereto with an incredulous shrug
of the shoulder. *Krafft-Ebing*, in the 7th edition of
his *Psychopathia Sexualis*, writes only about masturbation during early childhood and in the absence
of a peripheral exciting cause he regards every
manifestation of sexual life at that age as a sign of
neuropathic heredity, a contention that, according
to the present writer's view, is by no means true of
all cases. *Lombroso* writes only about children who
masturbate at the early age of three to seven. In
an interesting essay that appeared under the cap-
tion, "Anthropology in the Service of Pedagogy"
(*Die Zeit*, 1895, No. 27), he mentions superficially
the sexual life of children. Therein he states: "In
children from three to four years of age we may
observe also the first indications of the tendency to

  * *Über Coitus im Kindesalter. Eine hygienische studie.*
Wiener Mediz. Blätter, XVIII, No. 16, April 18, 1895.

the secret habit, naturally in a form limited by the incomplete development of the respective parts."

Zambuco describes a seven-year-old girl who carried on sexual deeds with boys and who was a victim of perverse sexual cravings. *Fürbringer*, in his recent work, *Die Stœrungen der Geschlechtsfunktionen des Mannes* (Disorders of Man's Sexual Functions), traces erections to the 15th year, on the average, *i.e.* the onset of puberty, but, like *Curschmann*, he has observed masturbation in children of five and younger ones. No reference is made to coitus among children.

Henoch, in spite of his rich experience, mentions no case. On the other hand he refers to the rhythmic motions of the pubic region which he has repeatedly observed in very young children and which he regards as an expression of onanistic excitation. A single observation (*Henoch, Kinderkrankheiten*, p. 220) meets our observations. A seven-year-old boy, Karl A., since his fifth year, as the result of sleeping for a long period with a relative who roused him by playing with him in bed, suffered of sleeplessness, enuresis, drowsiness and was addicted inordinately to masturbation. Unfortunately the age of the relative is not mentioned nor is it stated whether the boy only masturbates or was led to coitus.

Personal experience, clear memory and accident have led me several years ago to investigate this problem, so important for the hygiene of childhood.

If a large number of intelligent persons are questioned on this matter, if they are requested to try to recall carefully whatever they can, nearly every other person will be found able to recall certain incidents of early childhood, which were not understood before, but which upon closer scrutiny prove to be the earliest manifestations of the sexual instinct. Cases of actual coitus are rather rare. Usually we are told of mutual touching of the genitalia producing in the children an unusual measure of pleasurable feeling. Often the mere view of the genitalia, accidentally, as during play, is enough suddenly to arouse in boys (and only from them is a frank confession to be expected) a hitherto unknown sexual feeling. Childhood is the period which shows clearly that much of what human beings think they do through will and reason, is really done through instinct. Childhood is the bridge that links *homo sapiens* to the animal realm. Thus, *Lombroso*, for instance, sees in every child certain marks of the criminal, because during its earlier years the child represents the lowest type of man just as the fœtus during the first months stands for a lower animal species.

Thus coitus is discovered—instinctively—during childhood, mostly by the children themselves, on the path of the sexual instinct. Cases of children mishandled by adults are well known, of course, but these are outside the range of our present theme.

Whether during rape or repeated coitus a complete *immissio penis* takes place is doubtful. Usually the sexual act is carried out upon the vulva. But some of my observations appear to indicate a partial *immissio penis* into the vagina.

The possibility of this is not to be denied *a priori*. The child's erect penis by no means lacks the requisite stiffness. The hymen may be in a rudimentary state of development, or it may be of a so-called annular form. I have never been able to verify the presence of an actual hymeneal rupture and know of no positive histories of local pain, hemorrhage, etc. In certain villages—so a student informed me—coitus among children is a very common occurrence. He has frequently observed children who, left to themselves, carried out coitus in the fields at a very early age and considers certain vaginitides traceable to this cause. *Hoffmann* (*Gerichtliche Medizin*, p. 115) points out that in most cases of rape involving children the hymen is found intact. May it not be so richly endowed with elastic fibers as to oppose no great resistance to the penetration of the slim penis of a child? According to *Hyrtl* (*Topographische Anatomie*) the strength of the hymen grows with age and in old maids it grows stiff and leathery.

The children, who instinctively discover coitus, seem also in some remarkable manner to realize that they must keep this discovery secret from their

parents. Therefore but few cases come to the attention of the practitioner, who, unacquainted with
these facts, often fails to warn the parents in time
or to point out to them certain precautionary measures. Often coitus, or the awakened sexuality, is the
cause of an early start in the masturbation habit.

Coitus in itself appears to cause no particular
damage to the children's health. A number of my
cases of this category relate to healthy and strong
as well as to neuropathic subjects.

Here I interrupt the reproduction of this little
study. I may mention only that a number of observations are introduced to prove that the practice in
question involved perfectly healthy persons and that
it is a common occurrence which the physicians heretofore have uniformly overlooked.

The first case which I recorded in the study mentioned above, a boy who at four years of age carried
out coitus with a girl companion, seemed to most
physicians nothing less than a monstrosity. But
since that little study of mine was published, over
twenty years ago, I have become more thoroughly
familiar with the status of the matter. I have
queried numberless normal persons regarding their
early sexual reminiscences and all my earlier professional observations have been richly corroborated. I
know some cases in which the first attempt was made
between the second and third year. These children

grew up to be highly intelligent, cultured, noble minded persons. . . .

Notwithstanding all that, other physicians have failed to acknowledge the presence of sexuality during childhood. What may be the reasons for that?

In the first place there stands forth the fact that all persons endeavor to forget their own sexual past, insofar as it reaches back to the period of childhood. We are latently striving for innocence. We feel an urge to diminish the sense of personal guilt. We emphasize readily the educational errors, the sins of youth, of which we were the victims, in order that we may shift the responsibility away from us. We do not care to dwell upon that period of our youth during which all the primeval instincts of mankind struggled for supremacy within us. These manifestations we do not recognize in children, because if we did they would remind us of our own early life.

The repression of our own infantile sexuality leads also to the oversight of sexuality in our children,— in all children. In that respect we behave like the surprised country visitor who stands before a rhinoceros at the zoological garden and finally exclaims: "Nonsense! There ain't no sich animal!"

No! Most physicians are unacquainted with infantile sexuality for the reason that they cannot bear such knowledge. What is to become of all the current notions about the "purity" of childhood and about the "innocence" that well brought up children are supposed to preserve? Shall we always be reminded how clearcut our relations are to nature, to the animal world, and to the criminal?

Another reason for this phenomenal oversight may be seen in man's attitude towards the problem of personal responsibility. The establishment of social relations became possible only when the individual's self-consciousness was enlarged in favor of the social group. Religion made the strong weak by burdening him with the sense of guilt. Sexuality stands forth as the symbol of guilt, the emblem of sinfulness as a whole. In paradise man lived asexually, until the snake seduced Adam and the latter tasted of the tree of knowledge. Thereupon divinity drove him promptly out of paradise lest he should taste of the tree of life. Otherwise man would become immortal and a god. That means, he would become capable of enjoying sexual pleasure without the sense of sinfulness. . . . All discipline of cultural man rests on this feeling of guilt and on the fear of punishment. Man feels himself a weak sinner. . . .

We want the child to outgrow us in development. We want the child to attain the heights we were unable to reach, because our strength failed us. The child must fulfill the vision of our great historic mission, he must quench our thirst for glory. If we ourselves cannot be gods, we want our children to be god-like. The child must preserve the purity which was denied us. The child must uplift and sanctify us. Sinful parents often dedicated their children to the priesthood. This is the primitive expression of a wish we share alike, *viz.* the wish to make the child holy. Thus it comes about that the parents' belief in the purity of their children assumes ridiculous proportions. I have known of mothers physically assaulting the physician who informed them of the unexpected pregnancy of an unmarried daughter; I have known intelligent mothers to swear that their grown-up sons were wholly innocent and knew nothing of such "vile things," while the sons in question already possessed a large store of experience. All the obvious excitations of sexuality are belittled as accidental, as innocent play, as distant instinct. The child is something holy, pure, and noble, to the mother. Every mother feels herself a Mary who has given birth to a savior. She may admit as a last resort that possibly other children may be degenerates at an early age, but her child is a remarkable exception.

Yet in truth all children are alike. Only the forms differ under which sexuality manifests itself.

It is untrue therefore that our sexual life begins only at puberty. It is untrue that children become acquainted with sexual excitations only by being seduced or through the example of others, or that it depends on education alone whether a child is precocious or retarded in sexual matters.

Children start the practice of onanism during the first few days after birth! In most cases there are noticeable slight rhythmic swayings which thus disclose early the relationship between rhythm and sex. Before long the hand reaches down searchingly and finds the genitalia. Sometimes sucklings display erections immediately after birth. Every experienced midwife is able to corroborate this observation. I myself have observed erections occurring within a few hours after birth. The sucklings carry out onanism in various ways. Many, as soon as their hand is free carry it down to and stroke the sexual parts,—boys the penis, girls the clitoris.

Besides the genitalia all the other erogenous zones of the body serve as sources of auto-erotic gratification. "The whole body," states *Marcus*, in his excellent study, *Ueber verschiedene Formen des Lustgewinnung am eigenen Leibe*,[3] "may serve as a pleasurable source and this form of gratification is the most common. The child derives auto-erotic pleasure through the aid of the whole peripheral nerve system by suckling, by means of all sorts of muscle plays, through the excitation of the skin, stimulation of the urethra, of the anus, etc. Nevertheless I hold that even during earliest childhood onanism is already most commonly centered upon the genital areas proper."

The onset of the orgasm is not clearly observable

[3] Zentrbl. f. Psychoanalyse. Vol. III, p. 225.

in all cases. It seems to me that there are two types: children who experience a sort of permanent gratification (*Freud's* forepleasure [4]) and children who indulge intermittently in onanism and experience orgasm at such times. Many problematic "spells" in children and particularly in sucklings, the well-known "fainting" spells, or "absences," are nothing but manifestations of infantile onanism. Among the Europeans the infants are often bundled in tight swaddling clothes, and they are unable to reach their hands down to the genitalia so that parents and nurses are the more likely to overlook the rhythmic motions and the onanistic character of the habit. The onanistic spell usually begins with lively motions of the pelvic region; the legs are moved up and down; or the muscles are held tense, the thighs firmly pressed together; the breathing is hurried; the eyes are glassy and have a far-away look; the cheeks redden; and the orgasm is gone through in the midst of all sorts of twitchings, or with outcries and sighs, the breathing is labored or stertoric, and the child may turn blue in the face. The parents never appre-

---

[4] "It seems to me not unreasonable to fix by distinct terms this difference in the character of the pleasure through the excitation of erogenous zones and of that obtained through the outpouring of the sexual substance. The former may be called provisionally *fore-pleasure* in contra-distinction to the end-pleasure or gratification sense of sexual activity. The fore-pleasure thus is what the infantile sexual instinct is already capable of yielding, though in lesser measure; the end-pleasure is new, probably depending on developments which arise first with the onset of puberty."

ciate the true character of these spells and as a rule they protest most vehemently when the onanistic nature of the condition is explained to them. The physician is called in usually after the spells, he seldom has the opportunity to witness them and he may overlook the fact that such spells are but particular forms of the autoerotic orgasm.

Various spasmodic spells seen in children and regarded as epileptic, are also but equivalents of onanism. We may always recognize the two forms: a progressive orgasm followed by release of tension or a lightly accentuated but more or less permanent orgastic state.

Freud also holds that all children masturbate, and in his famous *Three Contributions to Sexual Theory* he recognizes clearly enough this standpoint. In the masturbation of infants *Freud* sees the first onanistic period, which does not last long and is followed by a period of latency when the practice is given up entirely. Although this account does not cover all cases, on the whole it is fairly correct. We find that the onanism of sucklings is soon given up. The girls cease carrying their hand to the pudendum, the boys no longer rub their genitalia. But I question whether the practice of onanism itself is abandoned. The children already show the influence of teachings and admonitions by the elders. The nurse slaps the child's hand disapprovingly, exclaiming: "Shame, must not do that!" Therefore the children begin to hide their doings from their parents. They give up masturbation of the genitalia but turn to other erogenous zones as sources of gratification. Cryptic onanism takes the place of the open practice.

I do not therefore accept the notion of a period of latency proposed by *Freud*. I hold that onanism persists continuously with but brief pauses. But I must add: a period of apparent latency comes more clearly to light in the neurotic than in others.

A series of carefully observed cases have furnished me the proof that onanism may persist throughout life,—without any period of latency. Where latency is prominently apparent it is a product of repression,—it marks specifically the beginning of the neurosis. Further on, when discussing the therapeutic measures, I shall point out to what a tremendous extent the child is harmed by the summary proscriptions of adults.

Freud expresses himself with a certain reserve regarding the period of latency that follows the onanism of sucklings and he admits that there are exceptions.

Briefly, there is no such thing as an asexual child. I said that sexual life awakens during the first days. It manifests itself as onanism and as a pleasure sense in connection with every form of erotic gratification. Suckling at the maternal breast is certainly an erotic act and in a certain sense so also is thumb sucking, which sometimes leads to orgasm. But I do not

consider all sucking and like motions onanistic. The
child merely preserves the inchoate pleasure-sense in
connection with all bodily excitations. His libido is
roused on all sides. He finds himself immersed in a
libidinous spree which is fairly continuous. Pleasurable innervations are roused around the genitalia,
the mouth, the anus, over the whole dermal surface,
and these are not yet perceived as either forbidden
or sinful. It is an orgy of sensorial gratification
such as the adult cannot forget. Therefore, we find
among the neurotics so many persons who have not
yet outgrown their suckling period, persons who
yearn after it and who imitate the state, I call them
ewige Säuglinge,—eternal sucklings!

Education intervenes and starts with the dis-
couraging doctrine that life is not made up of a
sequence of pleasurable sensations but that it means
a chain of duties. The process of repression starts
in then and there inasmuch as the pleasurable excitations of childhood which conflict with cultural
requirements, such as the child's coprophilia, are not
tolerated by the environment. The great struggle
sets in between narrow selfishness and social requirements; this struggle starts in the cradle.

At this point I want to emphasize once more:
Early awakening of sex is not exceptional but the
rule. Coitus and onanism during childhood are
signs neither of degeneration nor of depravity; on
the contrary, they are often merely the signs of the

budding forth of a keen spirit, and disclose a strong natural endowment such as always has its roots in a healthy, primordial instinctive urge.

Parents who come to me with the complaint that their child, they have discovered, is sexually roused and is given to the habit of onanism prematurely I reassure as follows: that may be a proof that your child possesses an extraordinary endowment and merely shows that strong energies are already displaying themselves.

I must not forget to add that not too rarely the reverse may also be the case: abnormal children, those who carry within themselves the roots of some serious psychic disorder, not infrequently begin to masturbate very early and most inordinately. Subsequently the mental disorder is thought to be due to the habit of masturbation, whereas that uninhibited outbreak of instinctive craving was already a manifestation,—an early symptom of the oncoming disorder. But such children show also other signs of degeneration,—delayed mental development,— whereas children who masturbate but who are not psychopathic frequently prove themselves precocious.

Nevertheless the diagnosis is at times difficult and only developments during subsequent years may disclose the true state of things. What we must do in such cases I shall point out elsewhere in the course of this work. For the present I only want to empha-

size the fact that under the inhibitions imposed by
the environment, masturbation is carried on as a
clandestine practice, but that it usually assumes
forms which I have called larvated, or cryptic,
onanism.[5]

But thus far I have referred to onanism exclusively as a normal manifestation even though this
work is dedicated to a description of the aberrations
of the sexual instinct. If one could only tell where
morbidity begins and where what we call normal has
its limits! Perversions are considered abnormal
manifestations; yet they are widely prevalent among
the primitive peoples, so that, fundamentally, perversions are "natural." But our age regards them
as morbidities. "Normality," or "normalcy," has
never been more highly prized than nowadays, yet
never has more of what is abnormal, *i.e.* repulsive,
been practiced for the sake of "normalcy" than in
our age. Nature inspires me too much with wonder,
for me to undertake to correct her processes or to
label her manifestations as morbid. My task must
be to prove that much of what we consider morbid is
natural and that back of our attempt to improve on
nature through coercion there is a great deal of
morbidity.

For that reason, in this work I shall not make use
of the ugly epithet perversion, but will use, instead,

[5] *Über larvierte Onanie.* Sexual Probleme, Vol. IX, No. 2,
February, 1913.

the term proposed by *I. S. Krauss: paraphilia.* This term fits better into my system of principles. Specifically I regard all the so-called perversions as parapathies, *i.e.* disorders of the emotions. Paraphilia, therefore, is a particular form of parapathy. Psychoses I call paralogies.

These points I bring out for the benefit of the reader who otherwise might find confusing the use of the new terms, paraphilia, parapathy, and paralogy. A new conception requires a new nomenclature that shall leave behind the odium with which sexual life has heretofore been regarded. The so-called aberrations and degenerations are mostly but variations of a single instinct. And the present book gives an account of the conditions which the moralists heretofore have described jointly as "degenerations" and as the "consequences of degeneration."

From that standpoint I could not begin more appropriately than with an account of onanism. Regarding onanism what antiquated views still prevail among our physicians who follow *Krafft-Ebing*, *Bloch* and *Forel* and who, in sexual matters, are not more enlightened than well-informed lay persons! And even famous sexuologists, like *Rohleder*, refer to onanism as a "degeneration" and supply an exhaustive list of dangers which they ascribe to the practice, as well as a similarly endless list of utterly useless prophylactic and therapeutic measures supposed to "cure" the evil once for all!

What I propose to do is to make my way through this wilderness of misunderstanding and to introduce into this important realm an unprejudiced logical viewpoint.

Possibly my effort will remain futile and for a time I shall probably be repaid with derision and scorn for my trouble rather than earn recognition or stimulate a desire on the part of others to test out my views. Nevertheless I shall fulfill my duty as an earnest investigator, knowing that no greater or more important duty confronts one.

Since the psychic disorders of the sexual function are my theme I should have perhaps not begun my inquiry with the subject of onanism. The practice of onanism is alleged to cause an endless series of physical disorders and through these the mental mechanism is alleged to suffer injury.

But I maintain: All the injuries ascribed to onanism exist only in the physician's fancy. All the alleged injuries are artefacts, they are the consequences of the prevailing system of morals,—a system which for two thousand years has combated sexuality and all pleasure-seeking.

But more of that later! Every one knows the meaning of onanism, yet there are no end of definitions and classifications, no end of attempts to exclude this feature or include that,—such is the pathway of science! *Rohleder* [6] defines: "We designate

[6] *Die Masturbation*, 3rd ed., Berlin, H. Kornfeld, 1912.

as onanism any form of activity of the sexual instinct whereby the external genitalia are excited, not as in Coitus, by the apposition and mutual friction of the male and female genitalia, but by the hand, or through some mechanical means, until the highest point of sexual excitation is attained in the female, or until ejaculation of the spermatic fluid is achieved in the male."

This definition is neither correct nor sufficiently comprehensive. It does not include the widely prevalent form of psychic onanism, during which the genitalia proper are not involved; it disregards onanism involving other erogenous zones (for instance, mechanical excitation of the anus), furthermore it stamps as onanistic the pleasure yielding of a sexual partner if secured through mutual excitation.

I consider auto-erotism, the expression proposed by *Havelock Ellis*, preferable to the antiquated and abused term, onanism. In a strict sense I regard onanism as nothing more nor less than auto-erotism. Onanism is an asocial sexual act. That is its chief characteristic. Men who cohabit with women for whom they feel no particular libido are not masturbating, as many authors maintain. I recognize no mutual onanism between two men or a pair of women. My definition, consequently, is as follows: Every sexual act carried out without the coöperation of another person is onanism.

This does not include the processes of phantasy.
For auto-erotic acts are seldom carried out in fancy,
because usually one or more persons are woven into
the picture as the objective of the gratification; ex-
cepting, of course, the rare cases, in which the
dreamer's own body becomes the object of his fancies,
—a feature of narcissism (the state of being in love
with oneself, the typical erotic egoism). Virtually
every auto-erotic act is a manifestation of narcissism. For the pleasure is derived from one's own
body. Moreover, close psychologic scrutiny of
human love relations discloses that every human
being seeks his self, or his self-reflecting image, in
others, and that every love, in a certain sense, is love
of self. We but love ourselves in others and hate
ourselves through our hatred of others.

We utilize the expression onanism, but we understand by it merely auto-erotism. How far would it
lead us if we called onanism every variation in the
love relations between man and woman or between
two men? According to my professional experience
coitus is not at all the rule even between married
couples. I know an endless number of cases in which
married couples or lovers indulge only in mutual
frictio genitalium instead of practicing coitus. The
reasons are various. Partly on account of the fear
of pregnancy, but partly also because in that manner
the orgasm is stronger for both.

It is also incorrect to state that two homosexuals

carry on mutual onanism. A sexual partnership is no longer onanism. Acts of that kind are no longer asocial,—they are the expression of a love relationship between two human beings.

These acts, characteristically enough, are but exceptionally felt by the subjects themselves to be onanistic. The odium that appertains to onanism attaches itself rather to the auto-erotic act. There is a deep foundation for that. The psychic processes during solitary onanism are wholly different from those accompanying gratification through a partner. Later on, in connection with the psychology of onanism, we shall have opportunity to go more fully into this subject.

We now turn our attention to the important question: is this auto-erotic activity harmful or not? But the matter hardly lends itself to a solution when put under the form of such a question. One might as well ask: is sexuality harmful or not?

Every so-called "normal" act may become harmful under certain conditions or when carried out in certain ways. Excess in food, drink, or sleep, many other physiologic functions when carried out improperly, or with excess, may become harmful. According to my professional observations, onanism, leaving aside the accompanying secondary mental states, ranks along with the so-called "normal" act in harmlessness. There are a number of forms of auto-erotic indulgence which lead to the excitation of the sexual glands and to disorders of the inner secretions. Therefore we must first acquaint ourselves with a sketchy survey of the various forms of onanism.

We may distinguish:

A. Onanism without mechanical excitation.

1. Through the generation of autochthonous fancies.

2. Through obscene readings.

3. Through lectures.

4. Through various affects,—chiefly through the outbreak of anxiety states.

The last form requires a few words of explanation. There are onanists who bring themselves into situations in which they experience dread and then ejaculation takes place accompanied by a powerful sense of gratification. A man of my acquaintance was in the habit of perpetrating a scarcely observable exhibitionistic act. This induced only a general tension. Thereupon there arose the phantasy that he is being watched by an officer. He would flee from the scene and the ejaculation followed. Another masturbated under the phantasy of not achieving some trivial aim. For instance he allowed himself but little time in which to catch a train so that he had to hurry at the last moment. This state of hurry was accompanied by the thought: *"you won't make it!"* It aroused a feeling of anxiety which increased rapidly until it led to an orgasm with all the accompanying manifestations. He could do the same thing while reading some favorite book. He would say to himself: *"You must get through reading in ten minutes. But lest you slight the task you must read aloud and pronounce clearly and distinctly every syllable!"* Placing the timepiece before him he soon would bring upon himself the anxiety state of not-coming-through until he achieved release through the orgasm. That man was hardly able to achieve an orgasm through ordinary friction. In such cases, too, he had to have recourse to some accompanying can't-get-there fancy before he achieved orgasm.[7] Similar manifestations may accompany other affects (anger, hatred, pity, shame, etc.).

We may distinguish further:

B. Onanism accompanied by mechanical excitation.

1. Mechanical excitation without the aid of phantasy. (This is a very rare form, inasmuch as the accompanying fancies remain for the most part "unconscious,"—a feature which we take up at length elsewhere.)

2. Mechanical procedures at the conclusion of day dreams.

---

[7] Back of this effect there lingers a *very definite* (cryptic) phantasy. Reduced to its nucleus the described case is traceable to a particular "paraphilia," which seemed unattainable to the subject. Inasmuch as the game was so staged that he finally reached the train or whatever he was after, the wish phantasy also ended in fulfillment, which expressed itself in the orgasm.

3. *Masturbatio prolongata.* The ejaculation is held back by the interruption of the mechanical friction or by the intrusion of anerotic phantasies. After an interval, the friction or the pleasurable fancies are renewed, but they are again stopped short of inducing the orgasm; in this manner the sexual act is protracted over an hour or longer!

4. A particular form is *masturbatio interrupta,* first described by *Rohleder.* In this form the orgasm is entirely suppressed. The onanist limits himself to the generation of the forepleasure and for hygienic or ethical reasons (loss of "seed," dislike of "uncleanliness") he renounces to the orgasm and the ejaculation.

C. Finally we must mention "unconscious auto-erotism." Various forms of spermatorrhœa—as for instance, during defæcation,—and pollutions, certain baffling spells which are followed by profound sleep (in children as well as in adults), absences, either brief or more or less prolonged,—these are but cryptic auto-erotic acts. In the case of pollutions the dreamer carries out either friction or the characteristic motions which induce orgasm. Defæcation is also carried out by such persons with the accompaniment of analerotic phantasies which may be unconscious. The spermatorrhœa is accompanied by a slight pleasurable feeling or merely by a tickling sense. Moreover we must point out that many persons are able to mask the tremendous end-

pleasure by enjoying the forepleasure in small libidinous instalments. The libidinous character of the
experience remains thus hidden from consciousness.

Such auto-erotic processes are very common; they
are, as a rule, very cleverly masked. Male adults,
for instance, may have no erections in connection
with them. They preserve the infantile forms of
pleasure so that the act of urinating, for instance,
stands for ejaculation (enuresis). Similar substi-
tutions may be traced in the case of sucking, nail
biting and various other muscular activities. In
actual life these procedures are not as clear-cut as
my reference to them in this connection might suggest, for there are numberless combinations and
transitional phases. For instance, I know a man
who pratices onanism first by conjuring up in his
fancy a scene of orgy and without the accompaniment of friction. Then he sets his muscles in strong
tension and thus brings on the orgasm. Others
attain gratification likewise while fencing, swimming,
cycling, or riding, through a combination of mechanical and psychic stimuli.

Everybody masturbates! No exception to this
is admissible, once we know that onanism may be
unconscious. The latter form may be called masked
or larvated onanism. I have already mentioned
some of its varieties. But the number is endless.
Here is a person, for instance, who is in the habit
of sticking his finger in the anus, ostensibly be-

cause he wants to loosen the indurated fæces. For the seeking of gratification via cryptic erotic means is always covered up by some plausible "reason." Another man considers himself subject to an eczema so that he must be constantly scratching his scrotum. Scratching the respective parts is common among those who suffer of hæmorrhoids who not infrequently emphasize the "sweet feeling" acompanying the itching and scratching of the parts. A third person, a woman, has a pruritus vaginæ, which likewise leads to inordinate scratching. After the orgasm the itching promptly subsides. Various mannerisms with the tongue, scratching of the skin, finger-boring the nose, and various tics, belong to this category. It is typical of these manifestations that the true character of the pleasure-sense is subdued so that it leaves the subjects in ignorance and the erotic nature of their gratification does not become disclosed to consciousness. In the case of males detumescence is left out entirely. The occurrence of erection would at once disclose the sexual character of the gratification. Even our medical practitioners are not yet aware of the erotic character of these forms of pleasure which are unaccompanied by erection. Spermatorrhœa is regarded as a special weakness of the sexual apparatus. This view is wholly contradicted by the fact that regular sexual intercourse is by far the best means of overcoming spermatorrhœa. Obviously when some other form of gratification is available spermatorrhœa becomes superfluous.

One may perhaps admit the universality of infantile onanism as a demonstrable fact and yet be inclined to deny the universality of the habit among adults. Let us leave aside the question of onanism during infancy and childhood and, for the present, let us turn our attention to the question: what proportion of persons beyond the pubertal age are addicted to the habit?

Earnest investigators calculate the number of masturbators to be 90% and over. Even *Rohleder* admits these high figures. Dr. *Meirowsky* placed at *Rohleder's* disposal statistical data which he had privately secured from physicians by means of a questionnaire. Among 88 physicians 78 masturbated,—88.7%. If we add thereto probable instances of cryptic onanism,—a form about which we shall write at greater length later,—we may confidently conclude that all persons masturbate. Nonmasturbators are exceptional. I have encountered a few cases of this type. They were extreme neurotics; and here, too, careful analytic research disclosed that each one carried on unconscious onanism. An educational-sexological survey in Budapest disclosed 96% onanists; of course I mean persons who have carried on masturbation at some time or other in their lives.

How widespread the habit is may be seen from a

relatively recent statistical inquiry by *Johannes Dueck* (*Sexual-probleme*, Xth year, No. 11) over 90% of those to whom the inquiry was sent, 90.8%, to be exact, admitted masturbation. Taking into consideration the cases of unconscious onanism, as well as some possibly false returns, for in such inquiries there are always a certain percentage of sanctimonious, holier-than-thou persons who testify falsely, my generalization does not appear in the least overstressed: everybody masturbates! Fully 75% of those who answered the questionnaire have testified that they have felt no evil effects from the practice.

Other investigators give the following figures regarding the prevalence of masturbation: *Marcuse*, 92%, *H. Cohn*, 99%, and *Oskar Berger*, 100%. What would be the present condition of the human race if that "awful habit" were actually as harmful as our busy-bodies and ignorant meddlers have tried to make out?

Of course certain onanistic indulgences are followed by various evils. We know that immediately after the act, or upon the following day, masturbators feel exhausted and tired out, complain of headaches and other pains, are unable to concentrate upon their work, etc.—a condition that *Ferenczi* has called one-day neurasthenia. But I am in a position to prove that this one-day neurasthenia is a psychogenetic condition. I have seen many persons relieved of this one-day neurasthenia as soon as they found out from me that the onanistic act in itself is wholly harmless and trivial and that only their fear made them anticipate the harmful consequences which were thus brought on through fear.

Consider the serious psychic struggle that the onanists undergo before they yield to the temptation of going through the act. They surround themselves with a thousand oaths, they try to protect themselves with prayers and resolutions, etc. They are strongly determined not to fall again! If they must yield—this one time,—let it be the last! And yet, in spite of all self-conjurations and in spite of all their resolutions, the instinctive craving persists within them and—there is a "next time," they yield once more; they slip back, again and again, in spite of everything. The spiritual *Katzenjammer* of defeat naturally brings on a severe depression. Consider also the influence of scare-books and of the well-meaning, but mistaken, efforts of teachers, parents and physicians, too, who are, alike, ignorant of the psychology of the situation! It has become part and parcel of our "enlightened" educational system to warn the child of the dangers of onanism. These warnings are positively more harmful than the habit! All such inhibitions build serious psychic conflicts. Religious, ethical, and hygienic counter-suggestions and advice,—all are alike cancelled by the power of the instinct! But after the orgasm

the inhibitions reassert themselves under the form
of self-reproach giving rise to that state of depression which even experienced practitioners regard as
the clinical picture of neurasthenia,—a disease that,
according to my professional experience, does not
exist at all, a label that will continue to serve as a
cloak for ignorance so long as the profession will
not take the trouble to look beyond and to differ-
entiate the psychogenetic conditions to which the
clinical picture in question specifically reduces itself,—such as anxiety neurosis, compulsion neurosis,
hypochondriasis or, in rare instances, a more serious
derangement such as dementia praecox, or cyclo-
themia.   If the harmless character of the auto-
erotic act is clearly explained, or if the masturbator
happens to have escaped the usual inhibitions, no
depression follows the practice; indeed, we hear repeatedly that after an auto-erotic act the subject
feels refreshed and relieved of morbid anxieties and
compulsions.

But for that, how would we explain such observations as the following?

A young man, 23 years of age, showing all the
typical signs of a severe neurosis confesses that for
the past two years he has given up the habit of
masturbation.   Since that time he suffers from
anxiety attacks and sleeplessness. *Freud,* as is well
known, has pointed out that masturbators become
victims of anxiety neurosis when they give up the

habit. They become unable to live without masturbating. Any physician is able to verify this
pertinent revelation. We find the most severe neuroses among those who give up the long-standing
habit. *Thereupon, through a process of false
reasoning, the neurosis is regarded as having been
brought about by masturbation. As a matter of
fact precisely the reverse is true. The neurosis is a
consequence of abstinence.*[8]

The young man who gave up the habit of masturbating and became seriously ill, he, too, was a
victim of abstinence. The harmless character of the
habit is fully explained to him, inasmuch as he is
not in a position to acquire a sexual partner and,
behold! The young man until now so seriously ill
gets well and shows no signs of neurasthenia and no
symptoms of any other neurosis!

I could give hundreds of such clinical observations
from practice. I choose from the data I have on
hand but a few typical illustrations which reveal
the same fundamental lesson. It is incredible that
so keen an observer as *Freud*, the investigator who
has disclosed to us the typical features of infantile
onanism, should arrive at the mistaken conclusion

---

[8] According to *Freud* masturbation is the cause of neurasthenia and abandonment of the habit leads to anxiety neurosis,
so that the poor neurastheniacs are left but the sorry choice
between neurasthenia and anxiety neurosis, unless they adopt
"normal sexual intercourse," a path which, as we shall presently see, is usually closed to them.

that masturbation causes neurasthenia, and should actually base his so-called actual neurosis,[9] upon that etiology.

Let us turn our attention a little more closely to a "neurasthenic" of this type and let us investigate whether the symptoms are truly brought on by masturbation.

Case One. Mr. T. O., docent in medicine, a foreigner, describes himself to me as a typical neurasthenic. He suffers—now in his 34th year—of terrific pressure around the head, which is usually at its worst in the morning and but gradually eases up in the course of the day. His digestion is very poor. He is generally constipated, must take cathartics, has no appetite and complains of a flat, pasty taste in the mouth. His food does not taste right. Whatever he eats is like straw and tastes likewise. He feels tired, exhausted and depressed. Often after walking up one flight of stairs he feels marked pains in the back, has palpitation, and is so tired as to want to lie down. He feels sleepy throughout the day and must keep himself roused with tea and black coffee. He wants to sleep all the time and when night comes he falls asleep readily but wakes up through the night and finds it hard to fall back

[9] *Freud* recognizes two forms of *actual neuroses* lacking psychogenous determinant, induced through physical disturbance of the sexual function: 1. *Anxiety neurosis* (caused usually by frustrated excitation, like *coitus interruptus*). 2. *Neurasthenia.*

to sleep. He has consulted already all the European authorities and they have always advanced the same diagnosis, saying to him: you are a severe neurasthenic! He has been in all the famous sanitaria, is a regular guest at a sanitarium for physical therapy, and has also tried vegetarianism.

As a cause of his trouble he regards masturbation, a practice to which he has been addicted inordinately since his eight year. He masturbated several times daily up to the period of his puberty, was in good health during that time, an expert gymnast and wide-awake young man, the best scholar in the class.

At about that time he heard that masturbation was very harmful and began to restrict the practice. He found it easy to limit himself to one daily indulgence, during the evening. If he tried to do without that one time, he could not fall asleep. He is not very clear about the accompanying phantasies. He always masturbated in a sort of half-sleep state, so that his hypnagogic picture merged into the dreams.

At 24 years of age he tried intercourse with women. He found that he was impotent, if the woman did not first rouse him for a time; after that extraordinarily potent. Soon he also found pleasure in sexual intercourse, which he at first had been going through without particular orgasm. But he must confess that the orgasm was never so strong

during coitus as during masturbation. The well
known statement of *Karl Kraus* held true in his
case: "Coitus is but a weak surrogate for onanism."
In spite of various love affairs which he carried on
before long he had to resort evenings to masturbation. Coitus also had a soporific effect upon him
and he has frequently fallen asleep in the woman's
arms. But in such cases he awoke with anxiety
whereas masturbation brought on four or five hours
of deep and restful slumber.

Four years ago Prof. X advised him to give up
onanism and to limit himself to intercourse with
women. This advice he has followed with an iron
determination. But it did not improve his condition. On the contrary, his nervous symptoms
date since that time. Before that time he was practically well, he was merely troubled by the thought
that masturbation may do him harm. He sought
the advice of the specialist who advised him to give
up the practice. The harmful effects of masturbation have appeared since. He read my contributions on the subject of masturbation and at once it
occurred to him that his condition is well described
therein: "I am neurasthenic," he said, "since I
have given up masturbation. But can you tell me
what my symptoms have to do with it? I cannot
see the connection."

I explained to our colleague how the head pressure
develops in the so-called neurasthenic. It is not a

toxic condition but the consequence of a continuous struggle within the head. The brain is the fighting ground between the rebellious thoughts which become clearly conscious and endeavor to transpose themselves into deeds, and the inhibitions of consciousness. This struggle becomes more violent at night. Hence the dread, when the rebellious thoughts threaten to come out victorious, hence also the feeling of lassitude in the morning, inasmuch as the struggle kept up throughout the night. And the condition is at its worst in the morning, because the thoughts endeavor to break into consciousness and consciousness is alertly on the defensive. But the unbidden wishes are troublesome also through the day. They again strive for that freedom of expression which they find, temporarily at least, during sleep, in the form of dream pictures.— Hence the drowsiness. The "subconscious" self strives for supremacy. One dozes off for a few minutes, so that the repressed wish may have the chance to take possession of the brain, if only for a brief interval. Such a state is troublesome; it robs one of all spiritual energy. Everything becomes subject to inner conflict. Persons in this plight find the world burdensome and they lose the joy of living; this shows itself as loss of appetite and constipation which, of course, are the consequences of that depression and of the slowing up of the metabolic processes.

"But what are my rebellious wishes? Why can't I sleep? What do I struggle against?"

"Against the inclination to masturbate. That of course is the superficial view of the situation. More correctly it may be said: you are struggling against that instinctive craving which onanism stands for in your case."

"I don't fight against onanism any longer. I did so, but now I feel no temptation."

"That is only the surface. The struggle is over so far as consciousness is concerned. But to the unconscious elements of your psyche it looms up more fierce than ever. Your trouble, the so-called neurasthenia, is an expression of the struggle. It is the evidence of a psychic conflict. Or have you other conflicts about which you have not yet told me anything?"

Thus our conversation proceeds, back and forth. The patient is not satisfied with our explanation. He feels that his current neurasthenia is a consequence of his abstinence, but he cannot understand in what manner or for what reason masturbation should be so indispensable to him. He enjoys women more than any of his acquaintances. I point out to him that the masturbation must be linked with some other sexual activity. He is urged to try to recall the phantasies on which he dwells while he masturbates.

When such a question is asked the answer one usually hears first is: "I always think (or thought, as the case may be) of a woman!" The specific and indispensable phantasy characteristic of the person in question comes to light only upon further inquiry.

So also with our patient. He reflected, then remarked with astonishment that before falling asleep he always saw the naked figure of a handsome boy and that dream and sleep followed this stereotypic hypnagogic picture. Further analysis revealed the presence of powerful homosexual cravings, which manifested themselves in a passionate love of boys; of these cravings the patient had not been consciously aware. This interest in handsome boys he felt only since his illness but to such a degree that he could fall in love with them. Never has he entertained the thought of meddling with a boy. . . . While saying this he blushes and I remark that some past scene has come to his mind. True enough! Last year at Ostend he saw a boy bathing and he watched that boy for hours; he also desired to open conversation with him. But just then he made the acquaintance of the boy's mother and she became his sweetheart.

He had transposed his homosexual interest upon the heterosexual path and had chosen the boy's mother, because she reflected the atmosphere of the beloved objective and he could easily identify the boy with her.

We see therefore that in this instance masturbation has a distinct function. It is for this man a substitute for homosexual indulgence which obviously he finds more pleasurable than the heterosexual.

The neurosis broke out only after the masturbation was given up because then the struggle against homosexuality became more open, whereas during the period of masturbation it remained upon the psychic level. In the company of women he was able to release only one component of his sexuality, the other he grappled with through the phantasy during masturbation.

His dreams and his behavior generally indicate that the neurosis is due to his pronounced bisexuality; that he is ill because he masturbates no longer and thus fails to pay the necessary tribute to his homosexuality.

One need only suppose this Dozent as engaged in the profession of teaching to appreciate that in such instances masturbation may be a protection to society.

In this connection the following case is significant:

Case Two. Mr. I. U., 56 years of age, is brought to me for examination on account of a criminal charge pending against him. He is a man with an abnormal, extraordinarily strong sexual craving. He began to masturbate during childhood and has kept up this habit down to his 53rd year. At 12 years of age he sought *puellae publicae* and at 13 he already had sexual relations with servant girls.

Nevertheless he kept up the habit and found it necessary to masturbate four to six times through the day before he could quiet down. Sometimes he found no rest any other way.

At the age of 53 he gave up the habit thinking that it might be harmful. But he had intercourse with his wife daily and in addition to that he sought the company of other women. He always masturbated with his mind on a specific phantasy: he played with little children, lifted their petticoats and carried on all sorts of childish games, which reminded him of a certain childhood incident. So long as he masturbated he was able to resist the temptation he felt of actually carrying out this phantasy. He insists that he has frequently had the opportunity to do so. Every large city has its regular childhood prostitution. The respective children easily recognize their prospective "friends" among the adults and acquaintances are readily made. He has had children offer themselves to him on the Prater promenade, in Vienna. But thus far he has been able easily to control himself. He would flee, hide in the bushes and masturbate. But he went to a country place and there a couple of children repeatedly roused him. Finally he became weak and yielded to the temptation. (The court found this alleged seduction by the children ridiculous as well as improbable. But I have the confession of a number of women who as children have done such

things and who have verified through their personal
experience the occurrence of such incredible incidents.)   Briefly he played sexual games with the
children because for nothing in the world would he
have reverted again to masturbation.   This passion
has him now in its clutches.   He is impotent with
his wife and he now has no other thought and nothing
else on his mind but children, and he feels that he
wants and must get them at any cost.   Finally
this brought him into the hands of the law and he
had to expiate for his misdeeds with a long prison
sentence.

Masturbation was a safety valve and a protection for this man.   At the same time it served as
a protection to society.

The next case seems to me even more significant:

Case Three.   Mr. W. V., 34 years of age, masturbates since his eighth year, with brief intermis-
sions.   He masturbates always with the phantasy
that he is overpowering and choking a girl.   At
14, a companion explained to him the evils of masturbation and also gave him a book to read which
contained a fearsome description of the terrible consequences of the habit.   He tried to give up the
practice.   During the periods of abstinence the
specific phantasy came to surface so powerfully
that he feared it might lead him to commit a crime.
He began to masturbate again and thereupon felt
more secure against his sadistic craving.   At 18

years he tried sexual intercourse with a *puella publica*, but found himself wholly impotent. Suicidal attempt at 21, following three months of abstinence. During that period of abstinence tremendously excited, pursued by sadistic dreams, and was shying from everybody, feeling uncertain of himself. Finally solved his struggle by giving himself up regularly to masturbation. Except for his morbid phantasies he now feels well.

Shall this man be dissuaded from masturbating when we know that abstinence would eventually provoke the commission of a crime?

In this sense masturbation plays an important social rôle. It serves to a certain extent as a defence, protecting society against the unhappy persons possessing overstressed instinctive cravings or insufficient ethical inhibitions. If masturbation were wholly repressed, the number of crimes against morals would become unbelievably large. On the other hand masturbation also protects certain masturbators against the commission of crimes. The masturbator stages his crimes only in his phantasy and remains socially inoffensive. Thus, autoerotism, an asocial act, becomes a social necessity.

Therefore, even excessive masturbation does not seem to me as dangerous as it is claimed to be. Our case histories inform us always of persons who fight masturbation and who break down under that yoke, and of others who give up the habit but become ill as a result of abstinence. Always the fear, the guilty conscience, the struggle is what turns out to be responsible for the masturbator's plight. I know a young man who has masturbated excessively for months. Every night he indulged for hours, ejaculating five to six times. He did not look badly and showed neither physical nor mental signs of trouble. He was an active, wide-awake young fellow who also gave promising signs of artistic talent. At my advice he gave up the habit and turned his attention to women. He was a sexual athlete, very lucky with women, but he had the misfortune of seducing a girl whom he was compelled to marry. He came to me after that already the father of a family. Although he had masturbated since his early childhood and indulged excessively during a period of months, as mentioned, he showed no ill effects. One might contend that this particular young man had an extraordinary strong sexual constitution. To be sure! That very constitution is what led him to excessive indulgence.

Masturbation is said to lead easily to excess. I have never known that to be the case. The sexual instinct cannot be suppressed. On the other hand it is not to be enhanced as easily as is generally believed. With the release of the libido, the incitation to indulgence is abated. Persons who masturbate often have a very strong need. How ridiculous it is to try to lay down rules in such matters! Our generation accustomed to being reglemented by medical proscriptions looks for rules regarding frequency of sexual intercourse. There are no rules! Everything depends on particular needs. I know married men who have carried on sexual intercourse daily for years, others who are satisfied with very little. I have never found that frequent intercourse affects longevity. A strong instinct requires more powerful expression. I have always found that persons become ill when they thwart their inner nature or requirements as they are often compelled to do for a great variety of reasons.

And there are persons actually unable to get along without masturbation. Deprive them of the indulgence and life itself loses all interest for them, as I have shown in my account of the suicidal impulse.

Masturbation is indispensable for many persons because for them it happens to be the only adequate form of gratification.

The specific phantasies are what render the practice of masturbation indispensable to those who have become accustomed to the indulgence. Very rarely are these fancies attainable in reality and when that actually happens they may in some measure become less imperative as fancies. Thus onanism stands forth as the only adequate means of gratification for many persons. We see this most clearly in homosexuality. The great significance of homosexuality in the neuroses and its rôle in our whole culture is a theme hardly touched upon by the older "learned" circles although the researches of the new psychology bearing on this problem are open to all who have eyes to see. There are many homosexuals who themselves do not suspect their condition: persons whose whole neurotic trouble represents but a flight from homosexual temptations. All such persons, no less than the overtly homosexual who for various reasons abstain from homosexual deeds, find in masturbation the only substitute which affords them a certain vicarious expression of their cravings. (In truth every indulgence in masturbation is a homosexual act and in the so-called normal person it serves as a means for releasing the never-absent homosexual trends.)

Many other forbidden yearnings find an expression and an outlet through masturbation. Consider only the various forms of fetichism, sadism, masochism and the asocial trends generally. Deprive these persons of their customary indulgence in masturbation and they go to pieces. It is easy to tell these sufferers: go to a woman, or seek a man. Many old maids, bashful widows, lonely bachelors find life endurable only through indulgence in masturbation, a practice which at least does not expose them to social dangers! I have advised many young people, as well as elderly persons, to seek "normal" sexual intercourse. In many instances such advice is useless because the male masturbators are impotent in the company of women, and the women find themselves anesthetic during the sexual embrace. But that is so not because the practice of masturbation has rendered them impotent, or anesthetic, respectively. Not at all! The fact is these persons are not seeking a sexual partner of the opposite sex at all. *Let us, once for all, abolish the fiction of normalcy in sexual matters.* A homosexual may marry and have children and yet remain ungratified, because he does not meet that form of gratification which alone would prove adequate in his case. Occasionally he breaks down under the burden of an anxiety neurosis and that disappears when he finds in the exercise of fairly active masturbation a substitute.

If masturbation were entirely suppressed the number of sexual misdeeds would increase to an immeasurable extent. Criminality would also increase very rapidly. I shall mention here but a single illustration. I know a masturbator who indulges in the habit with the phantasy of killing his father—of course, the phantasy being wholly unconscious. In his case the penis was a symbol for the father (*i.e.*, the procreator), the ejaculation stood for the blood stream which quickly drained the life of the procreator. The detumescence of the phallus symbolized the act of dying. And this is but one of the numberless phantasies at this

patient's disposal.   During masturbation he fancied
himself in all sorts of rôles, a condition like that
revealed by *Freud's* "penetrating eye" in the case
of the hysterical attack.   He was woman and man
at the same time (bisexual tendencies), playing,
therefore, an active and a passive rôle.   He could
play either rôle, according to the situations conjured up during his fancies, though usually he
played both rôles together.   Through analysis he
freed himself of these wild fancies, after they were
brought to light, and this cleared for him the path
towards woman.

Physicians unfamiliar with the devious paths of
neurotic fancies may be inclined to regard these
statements as ridiculous and phantastic.   Psycho-
therapeutists soon find out that their patients play
certain rôles and assume certain theatrical postures.
One subject is Christ, another Judas, a third one
Ahasverus.   Faust, the Flying Dutchman, Napoleon,
Gretchen, Ophelia or Messalina, and many others,
are types to be found among the neurotics.   The
stronger the cooperation of the phantasy, the
stronger is also the respective fiction.   I know
patients who play the rôle of the prodigal son,
carrying it out so faithfully that fiction and reality
have become hopelessly intertwined in their lives.
Every phantasy is richly utilized during masturbation.   I know a woman who plays the rôle of Desde-
mona; she always masturbates dwelling at the same

time on the phantasy of choking a black man.
Orgasm ensues at the moment of choking the life
out of her victim.

Another woman patient masturbated with the
phantasy of killing her mother. Later she reproached herself very bitterly. She claimed that
she had ruined her womb; that, through masturbation, she had hurt herself internally in some way.
That is why she had no children and was frigid
during her marital relations. It was a proper punishment for her great sin of indulging in the habit.
But note that the reproaches were not directed
against the onanistic acts proper; they were directed
rather against the accompanying phantasies. Hence
her hypochondriac fears, conjured up in accordance
with the principle of *lex talionis*, that she had hurt
her womb, etc. This shows us that the problem of
the feeling of guilt in connection with masturbation
is a complicated one.

Before turning our attention to the feeling of
guilt in connection with masturbation for the purpose of drawing the conclusions of interest to us,
let us first analyze a few individual cases at greater
length, and we must give closer attention particularly to the cryptic forms of masturbation. An
understanding of onanism will furnish us a better
background for the understanding of all paraphilias.
Most paraphilias are associated with onanistic acts,
i.e. they take place mostly in the auto-erotist's phan-

tasy. Frequently they are but aberrant and cryptic forms of masturbation.

Our most important conclusions thus far are:

1. *Masturbation is not the cause of the neuroses. The neuroses break out when masturbation is given up.*

2. *Masturbation owes its psychic significance to the accompanying specific phantasies.*

3. *When masturbation is given up the will to live itself is disturbed in many cases.*

4. *The mental and physical dangers of masturbation exist only in the imagination of ignorant physicians.*

Denken ist nur ein Verhalten der Triebe zu einander.

NIETZSCHE

II

Masturbation a Defence Manifestation—Nervous Disorder and Masturbation—The Neurosis sets in when the Habit is broken off—Case of an Abstinent Student—A Physician's Wife who read her Husband's Professional Books, Her Struggle against Masturbation, Her Suicide Letter—Suicide and Masturbation—Masturbation the Only Adequate Form of Gratification for Many Persons—Chronic Suicide through Masturbation—Masturbation and Incest—The Stammering Masturbator—Analysis of a School Boy who committed Suicide—Significance of the Specific Phantasy Associated with the Habit —A Case in which the Habit was due to the Fixation of a Phantasy—A Case of Masturbation— Consequences of the Habit—Physical Constitution and Masturbation—Transference from Masturbation to the Allerotic Form of Gratification—There exists no Norm for Sexual Intercourse—Various Criminal Phantasies of Masturbators—The Neurotic as Actor (Exhibitionist).

II

Thinking is but a relationship of the instincts to one another.

NIETZSCHE

In the struggle between instinct and repression, a struggle through which every person goes, masturbation becomes the representative of the conflict. The masturbator's guilty conscience does not always arise through the teachings of the so-called "hygienic" books, a class of literature that ought to be shelved. The masturbator's conscience has its autochthonous origin, because the habit involves a practice that conflicts with the ethical standards of modern culture. I regard conscience the sum of inhibitions which have arisen between "drive," or urge, and deed, or overt act. Conscience represents the endo-psychic recognition of the difference between individual predisposition and the requirements of cultural society. More plainly expressed: it marks the difference or tension between man's primal nature and his position as a member of society. The struggle against the criminal, selfish cravings of primordial man goes on without pause or intermission. Onanism becomes the symbol of all guilt, just as the sexual instinct stands forth as the representative of all primordial cravings. Very early the asocial and the sexual trends become closely linked because both belong to the mysterious realm of the forbidden.

The analyst is shocked to discover the primordial man in every member of cultural society. He shudders to find that every neurotic harbors much that is secret, asocial and cruel. And often he discovers that all forbidden gratifications must find expression through onanistic acts, if the neurotic is not to lose mental balance. How often passional crimes,—to mention but one category of instances—are never carried out, because through masturbation the sadist finds an outlet for his instincts in the realm of phantasy!

Thus masturbation serves to protect society against its own past. It fulfills an important social function. It protects the individual against the severe punishments of society as well as against social ostracism, and at the same time it protects society against the individual's asocial cravings.

I emphasize this fact not without compelling reason. Modern writers attempt to make a fine distinction between *Onanie* and *Onanismus*. *Onanie*, *i.e.* the temperate practice of auto-erotism, they claim, is harmless. Most all serious investigators admit so much, nowadays; but *onanism*,—intemperate indulgence,—they claim,—is harmful as well as dangerous! But where may the line be drawn?

Bloch, in his excellently written and well known work, states :[1]

"Generally speaking we can draw no line where harmless onanism ends and where the habit begins to assume dangerous proportions. Individuals differ and therefore their reactions are also subject to variation in that regard. *Curschmann*, for instance, mentions the case of a gifted writer, who in spite of indulging in the habit for eleven years, preserved his mental and physical health and kept up his literary activity with great success. *Fürbringer* reports a similar case of a College man. As in the case of sexual intercourse proper, masturbation is a practice subject to individual differences."

I am of the same opinion. But I also recognize the view that the evil effects are due to the psychic repression, and to autosuggestion as well as to suggestion on the physician's part. In the course of our clinical histories which follow we shall have frequent opportunity to revert to these matters. At this juncture I want to protest against the assumption that masturbation may be the cause of perversions, a view maintained even by *Bloch*. He states:

"The close relationship between perversions and masturbation is obvious. The stronger the habit, the more normal sensibility is blunted, the stronger and more peculiar are also the incitations required to bring about the orgasm. The sensuous images

[1] Sexual Life of Our Times, Rebman, N. Y.

must be varied more and more and before long they revert to the realm of perversions. Presently the perverse ideas become deeply inculcated and finally they assume the proportion of well-grounded sexual perversions."

In this connection reference is made to the *Tardieu* case, that of a man who masturbated seven or eight times daily, his phantasy dwelling on the outraging of female corpses, until it led him finally to the carrying out of his fancies, a distinctly sadistic outbreak. "He craved the sight of animal bodies slit open, dead dogs, he desecrated human corpses as a means for feeding his phantasy and of finding gratification for his morbid libido."

That illustrates the same faulty reasoning which in the past led to the misunderstanding of the relationship between masturbation and mental disorder. The sufferers masturbate because their inhibitions are removed. Masturbation, far from being the cause of mental disorder, is a consequence, a view which we owe to *Griesinger*. *Tardieu's* patient, was not led by the habit to his perversion; he masturbated because he was perverse, obviously always with the specific perverse phantasy, although he was probably unconscious of it. I shall give a number of such cases as illustrations. It is well for society that we do not know all the phantasies which accompany, consciously or half consciously, or unconsciously, every erotic indulgence. But on this aspect

of our subject we shall dwell later. We now return
to our present theme, the alleged dangers of masturbation, and I quote a few cases which show that
the giving up of the habit brings on some of the most
serious neuroses.

Case Four. Mr. H. D., medical student, 26 years
of age, writes me: "I have read some time ago your
essay on masturbation in the *Sexual-Probleme* and
found therein so much that applies to me that I have
decided to write you a little information about my
sexual life.

"Regarding sexual matter I was early a very
precocious child. The whole keenness of an awakened
child I turned early into sexual curiosity, specifically, trying as often as possible to see the genitalia
of those around me. The sight of a naked man,
or of a naked woman, gave me pleasurable thrills.
I recall such occurrences dating back to my fourth
year. Another incident dating back to my fifth
year remains forever imbedded in my memory. My
parents very improvidently took me to a dance.
There I saw a pretty woman in a red gown and it
made an unusual impression on me. I then had the
wish to lie naked in bed with her. For years I
thought of that woman. Always my thoughts of
her were accompanied with erections which began
early and which I experienced very frequently. I
was not happy like other children: always sad,
always dissatisfied, always in an expectant mood,

always with the unrest of one who hungers for something. I took no pleasure in any childhood games.

"My craving for love was boundless. As early as
during my sixth year already I fell in love with a
pretty little girl. While other boys played games, I
sat quietly near my beloved, stroking and admiring
her. To this day I cannot get along without a love
objective. I must always have some ideal and be in
love.

"At 12 years of age my school comrades taught me
to masturbate. I was inordinate and masturbated
daily, often several times daily.

Between my 14th and 15th year my father caught
me at it. He censured me severely, telling me I
will make myself very sick, also that I will become
insane if I don't give up the habit. My whole
vitality, he said, was being drained out of me through
the loss of semen. That scared me; I gave up the
habit and for a period of six months I abstained.

*During that time I acquired a fast heart, suffered
from anxiety attacks, became very excitable, and
slept very poorly. Up to the time when I gave up
masturbating I had been very well in every respect
and there was nothing the matter with me except for
my subdued temperament.* After that I had anxiety
over my school tasks and always pollutions in connection with the anxieties. Besides that, I had so
many nightly emissions that I preferred to masturbate again. I was sexually so excited at the time

that I felt like masturbating day and night.   At the same time I was a splendid scholar and showed signs of an extraordinary memory.   If I saw a three-page long poem once I was able to recite it and knew the position of each line.   The most intricate problems in mathematics I could solve in no time.

But now my struggle against the habit began once more.   My health soon gave way.   I suffered from headaches and palpitations.   My brain seemed burned out.   At night I suffered terribly from a tenesmus.   Every little while I had to get up to try to urinate.   I felt all the time tired and ill-disposed and sick of life.   Masturbation I restricted as much as possible but I did not give up the habit altogether. At 16 years of age I had the chance to cohabit with a servant girl.   My *potentia* was very good; I had intercourse with her many times that night.

The following morning will always remain unforgettable in my memory.   I felt like a new born being. My head was clear, my disposition pleasant,—the whole world seemed to me like paradise.

But, unfortunately that happy state did not last long.   The girl disappeared out of the house on the same day and my struggle against masturbation began once more, with all the terrible consequences. At 18 years of age I felt exhausted and as weak as an old man.   I consulted physicians and told them of my troubles.   Every one recommended abstinence. I was given bromides, cold water treatments, and valerian, and every one recommended regular sexual intercourse as the only remedy. It scared me and I gave up masturbating. Then my nervousness reached its worst stage. I became seriously depressed, and entertained thoughts of suicide. Nothing that I undertook was a success, everything was a source of trouble and worry. I suffered from continual headaches, and was so irritable that no one could get along with me. I began to feel unsteady, the very first thing in the morning, my limbs shook like an old man's. I could not concentrate my mind, I was always distracted, always absent minded. I had a feeling, as if the whole body, especially my mouth, was burning, or poisoned. In addition to that, the urinary tenesmus and the galloping heart.

I could never stay quietly in my room, I was always running around, and always in the company of girls, for whom I felt an ideal love. (Any girl whom I loved ideally I could never "degrade" by treating her as a sweetheart. In such instances I was always impotent. Love of men always disgusted me and was something I could not understand.)

"Now that I was wholly abstinent, I began to experience again the profuse seminal losses of my earlier days. What good did it do me? Sometimes I went to bed and as soon as I turned around I had an ejaculation. Excitement also produced pollutions. My gait became unsteady, I hardly dared to look a man straight in the face. Above all,

I was afraid, afraid even of small children. Disturbances of vision (photisms), and diarrhea.

"It was before the final examinations. I had the opportunity to indulge in sexual intercourse daily with a girl in the house, over a period of three weeks. I set no limit for myself. My brain cleared up and I was again able to study and I passed my examinations with flying colors.

"But after that I decided again that I must be abstinent until marriage. Again I became as ill as ever and even worse. I thought I was lost, and believed that now, at last, I was paying the penalty for the masturbation habit. Your writing was the first thing that cleared the matter for me and it has made a new man of me. I now have regular intercourse and feel like a new born person. All the former hypochondriac notions have left me, and in every respect I am now more efficient than formerly. I recognize that all my energy has been wasted on a useless struggle. The sexual instinct was, of course, stronger than my will power. I had numberless pollutions, in spite of all the precautions. Now I have quieted down and I no longer look upon the past as the augury of an uncertain future."

This case is interesting in many respects. In the first place the young man succeeded to turn from masturbation to sexual intercourse very readily,—proof that the habit was necessary in his case; in the second place we observe that the serious neurotic

symptoms always developed only during abstinence.
He was a young man with a strongly developed
sexual urge, unable to get along without some form
of sexual gratification.

The next case is similarly interesting:

Case Five. Mrs. W. Q., a physician's wife, is
referred to me, because she had once attempted
suicide and has been for months in a state of serious
depression. She gazes blankly in front of her for
hours, speaks no word, refuses food, and is fast
losing weight. Moreover, she suffers from compulsive ideas: her children will die soon, she is not equal
to the task of bringing them up properly, her husband has not the right kind of a helpmeet in her, etc.
She relates that her trouble arose as follows:
She has practiced masturbation since her fourth
year, possibly earlier. But she remembers very
clearly masturbating during her fourth year because
at that time she taught another girl the habit and
thereafter they indulged in the practice before one
another. She had always been a precocious child
and was so clever in hiding her habit that it was
never suspected in the house. She felt instinctively
that it was something which she must keep from her
mother and older sister. She developed very finely
and was a healthier child than most of her school
mates. Her progress in school was also excellent.

She masturbated daily at least once, occasionally several times daily.

Thus she grew up, like every other girl, was interested in art, learned painting for a time, and had no particular yearning for love, inasmuch as she felt contented with her masturbation. At 18 years of age she became acquainted with her present husband and fell in love with him. They married after a prolonged engagement and during that period she was impressed by the fact that although she felt a warm attachment for her man, his kisses did not rouse her sensuality. She comforted herself with the thought that her love was "spiritual," while her masturbation fitted her physical needs. After marriage she continued the habit because her husband's embrace left her cool. She was pleased to possess him and gratified that he desired her so hotly, but she never experienced orgasm. Her husband once tried to rouse her by friction of the clitoris but she disliked it and begged him to desist. She felt shame. . . . (Always we find corroborated the fact that the feeling of shame centers around the zones most strongly erogenous.) She continued to masturbate secretly and devoted herself to her children, four in number, in spite of her failure to experience orgasm during her husband's sexual embrace.

She began to take care of her husband's professional library and found pleasure in reading through his books. She came across a book on the subject of masturbation. She did not know at first what this meant but she soon found that it was a form of gratification to which she had been addicted all her life. She read in that book that masturbation leads to terrible consequences. She was particularly scared by a statement, in connection with a clinical account, that "the awful habit had woefully shattered the health of this delicate child." Terrible consequences to the nervous and mental constitution were also described and she read that when the evil effects do not show themselves promptly they do not fail to appear in time. . . . Now it occurred to her that she was surely a lost soul. She had been happy and full of the joy of life till then, chirping like a happy lark all the day long and going through the heaviest labors with a smile. Now everything had suddenly changed. She became depressed, shut in, and her voice was no longer heard. She had not known any physical complaints before. Now she began to feel pains in her limbs, in the back, and her suffering became unbearable. She was firmly convinced that she must have hurt her inner organs in some way. The book plainly stated that severe pains, cramps, convulsions, hysteria, and even epilepsy, are among the consequences of masturbation. The pains now began to center around the pelvic region, becoming unbearable during the menstrual period.

She was firmly convinced that indulgence in the habit had made her ill. She resolved to masturbate no longer and kept to her resolution for about three weeks after reading the warnings. Then she was amazed to find herself masturbating during a state of half-consciousness. Great was her horror, and she now feared going to sleep; she tied a bandage around her pelvic region, and woke from sleep with a feeling of dread. Nevertheless her craving was supreme and she felt herself giving in. She did not bear the thought of confessing to her husband. He held so lofty a view of woman's purity that he would have scorned her and possibly would have left her. But she loved him passionately and could not live without him. In her dilemma she decided she must die, took a large dose of veronal, and wrote her husband a parting letter, which I reproduce below as a touching document illustrating the depths of human suffering. She withstood the effects of the serious poisoning, and came out, after a slumber of thirty hours, without any serious consequences.

The letter was as follows:

My beloved Otto:
When you read this letter I won't be among the living any more. I pay with death for my wrong. I cannot keep on under the burden of a terrible habit, while you held me to be a pure woman. So, therefore, know: since childhood I have practiced masturbation. The habit began during childhood and I have kept it up after marriage. Finding myself too weak to give up the habit, unaided,

finding also that the consequences of the terrible habit already began to show themselves, and as I do not want to burden you with a sick wife, I part voluntarily and give up this life, though with heavy heart. Indeed, how shall I look you in the face, how shall I look my children in the face, when I find myself so badly dishonored and disgraced.

No! I cannot stand this any longer. For the love you have so richly bestowed on me, I thank you. I wish you the company of a woman worthy of your confidence and love. Do find a woman worthy of you. Kiss our dear children for me. It is hardest to part from you.

Forgive me. I cannot help it.

My last sighs go out to you.

Yours

. . . .

The husband, deeply stirred, promised to stand by her and to help her in the hard struggle. She, on her part, promised to inform him at once whenever she gave in to the habit. This promise, which to her was holy, protected her against further indulgence . . . but her mental suffering was most severe. She abstained from masturbating, but became sleepless, had weeping spells, reproached herself continually and was so badly run down physically that she had to be taken to a sanitarium. When the physician, after trying out all ordinary means without effect, found himself compelled to explain to her that her illness was not due to the masturbation habit, but that, on the contrary, it was the result of her abstinence, she lost faith in the doctor. She said to him: "Even if I knew that it would make me well I would not return to the habit. I have gone through too much, I am too proud now to go back to the old habit." Her husband, to whom she related the physician's statement and advice, made an angry scene over it and took her away from the sanitarium. Then she came to me and told me the events as I have just related them. The analysis, subsequently, revealed various fixations of the libido back of the masturbation practice. An accompanying phantasy which always centered in the following scene was revealed under great resistance:

She was yet a small child. A big boy came along and raising her skirt began to tickle her "privates." This phantasy proved to be the repetition of an infantile scene involving her brother, six years older than herself. There were revealed fixations on the family and homosexual tendencies. Great improvement after the analysis. At any rate I succeeded to relieve her of the great aversion she had felt against *frictio clitoridis* by her husband. That aversion was due to memory of the pathogenetic scene of her seduction. It was an unconscious thought-feeling, approximately: "If your husband but knew that your brother has done this to you and that you were not 'innocent' when he married you!" Her mind had differentiated between husband and brother. She was virgo intacta for coitus, but not for *frictio*.

A further determinant for her attempt at suicide was the fact that her brother married about that time and she could not be present at the ceremony because her husband and brother were not on speaking terms. However, after the analysis she found herself able to tolerate *frictio clitoridis* and experienced great orgasm through this means. She again found her gratification and that, indeed, was the most significant progressive step to which she owed her eventual recovery. Gradually she arrived at a saner view regarding masturbation and she found out that her fear had conjured up all the alleged evil consequences of the habit.

An examination of this case reveals two important facts: First, that ideas of suicide bear a certain relationship to masturbation. Already, years ago, I drew pointedly the attention of the medical profession to this relationship.[2] Second, the significance of the phantasies accompanying the act of masturbation.

Suicide represents merely the extreme consequence of abstinence. It is possible to construct a scale, approximately as follows: anxiety neurosis, hypochondria, moodiness, depression, melancholia, suicide. From the day masturbation is given up life ceases to be worth while for these persons.

The inexperienced inquirer may raise the question: why do these persons fail to find gratification upon

[2] *Vid.* my contribution to the Symposium on Suicide, *Über den Selbstmord, insbesondere der Schülerselbsmord.* Verlag, J. F. Bergmann, Wiesbaden.

the allerotic path?   Why do they not seek their
libido in normal sexual intercourse, or even in perverse acts with other persons?   Precisely because
masturbation is the only possible adequate form of
gratification for them.   I have already stated that if
we unearthed all the masturbator's phantasies the
unfulfillable character of their instinctive cravings
would fill us with amazement.   There are masturbators who indulge in the practice under the urge of
criminal phantasies, others who carry out perverse
acts, others again who indulge in imaginary orgies
which would require the powers of a Nero for their
actual fulfillment; finally there are those who dwell
upon a specific childhood scene; and untold numbers
dwell upon incest phantasies, of which they are not
conscious.   The masturbation act is preceded by a
sort of intoxication or ecstasy, during which the
current moment disappears and the forbidden phantasy alone reigns supreme.   The thing is over in a
few minutes, or seconds, then the curtain falls over
the secret and the light of consciousness is unable to
penetrate through that curtain.   These masturbators
play with and before themselves; usually their game
succeeds; they possess virtually a split personality,
one addicted to the habit of masturbating under the
control of some specific phantasy, while the other
personality cannot, or will not, or must not, know
anything about it.

We have seen that the neurosis breaks out as soon

as the masturbation is given up and that the consequences of the abstinence are then regarded as the result of the habit. It would be as proper to contend that masturbation affects the nerves so as to lead to suicide. I place on record cases proving precisely the obverse. These cases demonstrate to our satisfaction that many persons are unable to live without masturbating and that they would rather renounce living altogether than try to get along without their customary gratification.

Among the masturbators there also are very many who have read about, or had been warned against, the alleged dangers. Subsequently they practice the habit with the pride of persons who feel that they are masters over their own lives and who are ready to sacrifice their lives in that pleasurable form. Attempt at suicide through the abuse of masturbation is by no means rare; is a particularly frequent occurrence in jails. This form of self-annihilation I have called "chronic suicide."

It is not sufficiently appreciated that masturbation also serves as self-punishment as well as a means of shortening one's life. The linking of punishment and pleasure is a well known occurrence in the psychic realm. We need only recall flagellantism and the ascetic self-denials of the Saints. We shall point out presently the tremendous rôle of masturbation phantasies in connection with suicide. At this juncture I only want to emphasize that the

warnings by which parents attempt to scare children
away from the practice of masturbation frequently
have the opposite effect: some stubborn children
cling to the habit precisely because they mean to
harm themselves thereby and shorten their lives; for
their secret gratification they pay with the realiza-
tion that they dare sacrifice a part of their vital
powers in the act. The gruesome play with death
and the knowledge of doing something forbidden
merely enhance the gratification-value of the practice. Between chronic and acute suicide the line is
continuous and gradual. The antisexual instinct is
decidedly the life-denying instinct.

There are persons who have lost the courage to
love, who have been robbed of the joy of living
through the inhibitions and commandments inculcated by well-meaning but mischievous parents, and
such persons are unable to experience pleasure without a sense of guilt. In this connection I am reminded of a young girl who happened to be surcharged with a craving for love, a girl in whom
every instinct cried out for fulfillment but who had
been hemmed in with so many taboos and so many
inhibitions through an excess of moral cant that she
found herself completely thwarted and there was
nothing left for her to do but to renounce life. Her
fear of love was almost as overpowering as her
craving for it. She was too weak to yield to her sexual instincts: too "moral," too weighted down with

the cut-and-dried philistine morals. On the other hand without the fulfillment of her erotic inclinations life was not worth living and therefore she decided to cut the unsolvable riddle by choosing death.

At any rate this case proves that, as *Freud* has pointed out, suicides are often burdened with incestuous thoughts, and that such thoughts are usually the source of the most bitter self-reproach.

This girl, too, had experienced an incestuous trauma during her childhood,—a trauma in which her brother, too, was concerned. And perhaps her inability to love was due to that. She was too tightly anchored to the bosom of her family. In addition to the moral inhibitions the secret link that bound her to the brother robbed her of her freedom. She knew but one true love: the love of her brother, the first beloved, whom one never forgets. In the midst of that dilemma she chose death as a release.

But the analysis of this case reveals another important point which thus far I have found to hold true of all cases of suicide, or attempts at suicide, that I have had the opportunity to examine. This patient developed her suicidal ideas *only after she had given up the practice of masturbation.* The strict abstinence was one of the outstanding causes which led to the attempt at suicide in this case. We have learned already that masturbation becomes an indispensable practice for these persons, displacing in value even regular sexual intercourse, because it is

linked with various phantasies. *The self-reproaches
in which the patients indulge on account of the habit
are really directed against the accompanying phantasies.*

That was the case also in this instance. Through
her phantasies, the patient linked with her auto-
erotism the childhood experience in which her brother
figured. Giving up masturbation involved also giving up the accompanying incestuous phantasy. The
suicidal act, which fortunately proved unsuccessful,
was carried out after the girl had left her parental
home and when she found herself among strangers.
She swallowed a quantity of morphin and veronal,
but she vomited the mixture. The life instinct
turned against the suicidal effort. A voice within
her cried out: "You can yet be happy!" That
voice proved true. In a few years she met a man
who made her happy. It was an uncle who in many
ways resembled her brother.

Even more convincing seems to me another case,
an attempt at suicide by a highly talented artist
who obtained from a friend a large dose of potassium
and drained the mixture quickly with the certainty of
going to his death. The poison turned out to be but
an ordinary dose of potassium bromide and the poor
fellow woke up from a prolonged sleep with nothing
worse than a heavy head. This patient, too, suffered
from compulsions and suicidal ideas, and he was also
a victim of self-reproach on account of masturba-

tion,—a habit which he had carried along into adult age. His most serious compulsion was the thought that some one might try to commit an assault on him. Specifically a homosexual reminiscence dating back to his 9th year! The fear, in that connection, corresponded to the burning wish of finding the particular form of gratification which once roused his highest libido, because homosexuality was distinctly pleasurable. This patient had also gone through a severe incestuous trauma (with his sister) and in his case, too, the overwhelming thoughts,— which were chiefly of the nature of self-reproach,— responsible for the attempt at suicide, were found to have flared up with the giving up of masturbation. The fear of an encounter with some one corresponded to the wish for the return of his sister. His greatest wish turned into his deepest fear.

I want to record the case of another patient who masturbated till his 34th year. After he gave up his auto-erotic practice, he became a victim of suicidal impulses. In this case, too, analysis revealed very clearly the intimate relationship between the auto-erotic acts and incestuous phantasies. As a child the patient had suffered from bladder trouble. His anuria was easily overcome when his mother's hand stroked lightly his penis. During his masturbation act he imitated this action. Masturbation is but a return to some infantile form of gratification, a reversion back to the earliest sources of libido. His potentia was also irregular and sometimes erection succeeded only after a similar manipulation.

Another feature is significant in this, as in all such cases: All masturbation acts, in the last analysis, represent a compromise between homo- and hetero-sexual excitations (*Vid.* previous case). Particularly in this case it was very evident that masturbation stood for the incest phantasy as well as for a homosexual act.

Persons of this type are unable to endure life without masturbating. The habit, for them, is not, as previously mentioned, punishment and expiation, but it stands for secret gratification and associated with it then is a strong sense of guilt. That feeling of self-reproach, as the observations of many other physicians show, may become so strong as to lead to an attempt at suicide immediately after indulgence in masturbation. In that connection, next to masturbation, disgust plays an important rôle. Auto-erotists of this type regard their self-gratification as a "disgusting" and degrading act. Disgust with self becomes disgust with life,—with the whole world. Life, being always appraised sexually, loses its worth. The feeling of revulsion becomes supreme. In particular masturbators who have been abstinent for a time and who have thought that they have succeeded in fighting off the habit, after a relapse, which robs them of their last hopes of recovery, find themselves readily disposed to "lay hands on themselves" and with a supreme onanistic act, *i.e.* through suicide, they carry out the supreme act of self-punishment.

I want to refer now to the analysis of a boy, in whose case thoughts of suicidal thoughts played a great rôle. The complete history of the case will be found in my study entitled *Compulsion States, their Psychic Background and Treatment* (*Medizinische Klinik*, 1910, Nos. 5-7). A portion of the history is reproduced below:

CASE 6. In my work on *Nervous Anxiety States*, I have pointed out the psychic roots of stammering. A stuttering boy, whom I treated during the last few years, told me that his stuttering ceased whenever he held his nose. If he pressed the right index finger against the bridge of the nose he could speak fluently and clearly at once. This boy was an inveterate masturbator. His great fear was that he might be found out or that in some way his secret habit may show itself. His father once asked him to keep his hands always outside the covers while in bed. Consequently his father must have suspected masturbation. What was the meaning of the boy's symbolic act? If he held his hand in his pocket he could masturbate. With the hand on his nose he demonstrated before the whole world: Look, I do not masturbate, my hand is not in my pocket, it is on the nose! At the same time the nose was to him a symbol of the sexual organ and through this compulsive mannerism he disclosed as much of his secret as he tried to hide. The same boy suffered for a time from compulsive lying. One day he told me a lengthy story which I detected at once to be false. I asked him, point blank, why he lied to me. He excused himself, saying he could not help it, "suddenly it comes upon him, and he cannot help telling fibs." The previous day he had lied to his father, although there was no need of it. The teacher being ill, the class was excused from attendance. But when he came home he told his father that the class had been dismissed because they were repairing the roof of the school building. He could not explain why he told that falsehood. Was he glad that school was off for the day? "Oh, very."

"Then you really were glad that your teacher was sick instead of feeling sympathy for him, as a good boy would?"

That he readily admitted; he had often wished the teacher to be sick and he did not find it easy to hide this unworthy sentiment before his father. He also entertained the wish—disclosed by the analysis —that his father be ill. That goes deeper than the conflicts thus far exposed; we leave aside the closer motivations of this wish. But this was only one reason for the false statement. Another reason was that he wanted to test his father. He wanted to find out whether his father really "knew" everything, specifically, of course, whether his father was capable of discovering that he masturbates and that he secretly harbors "unholy thoughts."

This boy had previously gone through an unpleasant experience. He was under the care of a "Specialist for Stammerers," a man who had read my book in which I traced the relationship between speech defects and masturbation as due to repressed sexual wishes. As soon as he found himself alone with the boy that specialist took the boy's reflexes and then, looking him straight in the eye, said: "You are masturbating!" Of course that was the worst he could have done, especially since the boy suffered from the very fear that the whole world could detect this habit about him. It was precisely on account of that fear that he was backward in society and stuttered, in the presence of his mother, or his father; he stuttered, in fact, whenever any one was present, whereas, like all stammerers, when he was alone, he could talk fluently. Now that specialist strengthened his suspicion that his secret habit could be detected in him at a glance. Then, by his compulsive mannerism (pressing hand against the nose), he was demonstrating before the whole world that he was not guilty. I learned all that from him. Now, why did he lie to me? Just as he disproved his father's omniscience by his false report, he now lied to me so as to test me and find out whether I really could discover everything about a person, inasmuch

as I had told him concerning his inner life things
that nobody had theretofore suspected about him.
His tendency to falsehood was due to unconscious
"repressed" motives and therefore it assumed a
"compulsive character."

The case illustrates the whole secret mechanism
of the mind at work under similar circumstances:
The sense of guilt towards the teacher and father,
because he wished them dead, and the inhibitions
with which he was burdened. We may appreciate
that, in view of his inability to give up the habit,
suicidal thoughts necessarily broke forth.

I conclude these observations on the relationship
of suicide and masturbation with the report of the
analysis of an attempted suicide, the case of a school
boy, that seems to me to demonstrate very con-
vincingly the views I have brought forth.

CASE 7. An 18-year-old boy, Commercial School
student, went to school one morning, showed keen
interest in his lessons and an hour later shot himself
through the head with a revolver. The cause of this
suicide was apparently brought out without difficulty. The motive seemed to be: unrequited love.
During the two preceding months he had been in love
with a girl of his own age and had told his parents
that he was going to get engaged to her. Because
his parents were opposed to the idea and since he
felt unable to live on without the parents' aid,

according to his earliest account, he decided to take his life. After several weeks of invalidism he improved enough to leave the sick bed and soon afterwards he returned to his studies, completely recovered in health. The attempted suicide had scared the parents into acceding to his desire; but while he was yet lying ill in bed he noticed that his sweetheart lost her charm for him and therefore he found it easy and not at all a sacrifice to give her up after a few months.

He admits that the impulse to the deed was the thought of revenge against his parents. He regarded himself a lost soul, a man unable to think any longer and fast approaching the borders of insanity. All his life he had a great longing for tenderness, and an older sister was kind to him in that way. We learn that the letter in which his parents warned him of their refusal to approve his intended engagement contained also a few lines from his sister in which the latter expressed herself very emphatically concerning the hopeless character of his love venture. Shortly after receiving that missive he attempted suicide.

His sexual life, upon superficial scrutiny, shows no particularly striking deviations from the usual histories. Corrupted by comrades, at 15 years of age he attempted to get in touch with a prostitute for the first time and in this attempt he failed at first. During his seventh High School year he began to

masturbate, in that way experiencing a libido theretofore unknown to him. But he read various warnings against the habit, and, fearing that it shortens
life, he abandoned the practice. Thereafter he had
occasional intercourse with prostitutes and servant
girls. During the eighth High School year he masturbated only thirteen times in all. But he admitted
that his libido was never so great during sexual
intercourse as during masturbation.

Next we learn that in his case masturbation was
actually linked with incestuous phantasies. During
the very first indulgence in masturbation it occurred
to him suddenly that he would like to possess an
elderly woman. Suddenly, much to his horror, the
image of his mother came to his mind.

We now perceive why he gave up the practice of
masturbation. The accompanying incest phantasy
rendered the continuation of this form of gratification literally impossible. He recalled also various
occurrences which corroborated the incestuous attachment to the mother. High among the moun-
tains, while wandering, he met one day an old, ugly
peasant woman, and ugly thoughts came to his
mind, but these he promptly banished. Various
dreams were concerned with his mother and his
sister. We are told next that his relations with the
sweetheart had reached a very intimate stage and
might have led to serious consequences if his strong
inhibition had not prevented him from taking full

advantage of their intimacy, in spite of the sweetheart's willingness. He was in bed with her and in
spite of great desire and painful erections he did not
touch her. *He treated her as a sister.* He also
confessed having carried out various pederastic acts
with a younger brother.

The experienced psychotherapeutist at once recognizes that the attempted suicide was a case of
pœna talionis, of self-punishment. It was a letter
from the mother and the sister, pointing out the
hopelessness of his love affair, that prompted the
deed. The girl was identified with his sister, who
bore the same name, and through this identification
the hopeless character of all his incestuous phantasies were converted for him into a certainty. From
mother, sister, and brother he shifted the conflict
over to the girl whom he treated like a *noli me
tangere*,—as a sister.

But what was the reason for his attempt at suicide? Not the parental letter of refusal. Not the
hopeless character of his love affair, since he could
have easily possessed the girl. Not that,—only his
*deep sense of guilt—the insolvable character of his
mental conflict: his inability to carry on masturbation as a substitute for his incestuous and homosexual longings.*

We learn further that the first act of masturbation he carried out directly after visiting a prostitute,—a visit, to be noted, that proved successful.

It proves that reality could not satisfy him as well as the auto-erotic act with its accompanying incestuous phantasy.

The significance of the specific phantasy during masturbation cannot be emphasized too strongly. The feeling of guilt associated with the practice depends on that as well as on the intensity of the gratification. It is the specific phantasy that gives the act of masturbation its particular coloring, and its high pleasure-quality, rendering it irreplaceable by any substitution.

There are observations which bring these relationships plainly into view in the midst of our cultural state. The following is a case of that type:

CASE 8.   Mr. B. M. consults me on account of the following trouble: He had always been normal and, without masturbating, at sixteen years of age began having intercourse with women. From the 16th to his 28th year he had intercourse with various girls, women, prostitutes, without any particular trouble; his potentia and orgasm alike were vigorous. Then he became acquainted with a girl whom he liked very much. They understood each other and with her he could converse more satisfactorily than with anybody. Finally he proposed that she accompany him on a journey. She agreed and they had a beautiful trip, lasting six weeks. But his hopes of possessing

the girl were frustrated.   She went to bed with him;
but she shrunk back whenever he tried to touch her
and he could do nothing.   She wailed that he wanted
to ruin her.   He hoped to attain his end through the
exercise of patience and by artfully rousing the
girl.   But in vain!   Against the sweetheart's resistance all his efforts proved fruitless so that he found
himself reduced to masturbating while lying with her
in bed.

After the journey he tried to cool his ardor in the
company of other girls.   But he found himself impotent; could attain neither erection nor orgasm.
He had to masturbate daily and always the image
of the girl was before his vision.   When I asked him
why he did not marry her he answered:

"That cannot be.   We are too far apart socially.
She was a governess, a servant, therefore, though of
a higher class, while I am a college trained man, a
lawyer.   Besides, I have my mother and she would
never approve. . . ."

"Are you the only son?"

"Indeed . . . and my life with my mother is so
harmonious, so quiet, so beautiful, that I don't need
marriage.   I have decided never to marry.   But my
passion for that girl became so great, that I was
afraid I should marry her after all.   It occurred
to me to urge her to go to America and I gave her
the money for the journey.   She is now in the United
States. . . . Though she is so far away, I cannot

forget her. Her letters are getting cooler all the
time, but on my part I love her as ever and love her
more and more every day."

He carries on a bitter struggle against masturbation and admits ruefully that he always fails. . . .
Although he has physically improved during the
past four years and feels much better, nevertheless
he is afraid that masturbation hurts him. He fears
that his spinal cord and his memory are affected.
He would like to forget that love and to be able again
to possess other girls.

This case illustrates the power of an unfulfilled
wish continually pressing for expression. Such ungratified wishes never die. Had he married the girl,
depreciation would have followed the act of possessing her. . . . The strong orgasm during masturbation is induced by the image of the girl and by the
phantasy that he is possessing her. His phantasy
brings about fulfilment, the only kind of fulfilment
that he craves.

The only? A closer analysis alone might determine that point. It is very likely that back of the
girl stands the fixation on the mother. The girl and
the mother have much in common. Both are unattainable, both negativistic, from the standpoint of
the sexual wish. For the sake of the mother he did
not marry the girl, he did not want to leave his
mother. That proves that the mother is his stronger

attachment and we must regard his masturbation as
a regression to the pleasure sources of childhood.
He so arranged the relationship that it should remain distant and unattainable. He used no force
hoping the girl would yield willingly. But women
want to be taken by storm, so that they may have
for themselves the excuse of *vis major*,—coercion.
That step, however, he did not venture to take. Her
refusal was a source of great sexual excitation for
him; likewise the practice of masturbation at the
side of a beloved objective.

It seems to me superfluous to draw further inferences. The case is instructive because it displays
the significance of the phantasies accompanying
masturbation perhaps more clearly than any other
case.

The patient's statement about his physical condition is interesting. In spite of the habit he maintained himself in excellent health since giving up
regular intercourse. He has gained in weight and is
very active. Even after a night during which he
masturbates three and four times he feels no unpleasant consequences. Once he abstained from the habit
for a period of four weeks. He wanted to test his
power of self-control. But he found himself getting
so irritable and nervous that he could stand it no
longer. The whole household was in an uproar on
account of his irritability. He had had such severe

outbreaks of "nerves" even at night that it scared his
mother and she called in the family physician. The
doctor, upon hearing that the patient had had no
sexual intercourse for years, advised him to seek a
woman (about his masturbation practice the man,
naturally, said nothing); that, he was told, would
quiet him down. He again masturbated a few times
and in a few weeks he was again once more able to
sleep, finding himself, in fact, refreshed and quiet, on
the very day following the indulgence. . . .

Masturbation, for him, substituted the lost girl.
But the girl, in her turn, was only a symbol for the
mother. That I found out, a few weeks later, when
he came again to me and related a dream in which
the girl changed into the mother. He awoke with
terror, and decided to compel himself to have intercourse with other girls and to masturbate no
longer.

But he continued to be impotent with other girls.
He developed sleeplessness and a nervous trem-
bling. As soon as he stretched in bed his body began
to shiver and to shake. He was all a-quiver, like a
machine. Jumping out of bed he would pace the
floor back and forth, like one possessed. Finally he
said to himself: this time you masturbate if it cost
you your whole life. Then he would quiet down,
able, at last, to fall asleep. After resuming the
habit to a moderate extent his condition improved,

he was again able to work and finally he adopted himself to his more serious tasks.

I could quote hundreds of like cases. Let me mention briefly but a few that now come to my mind: A woman, perfectly well up to the time when she gave up masturbation; then, following abstinence upon the advice of a physician, melancholia. (She had consulted the physician on account of a trivial vaginal discharge.)

A physician; practiced the habit till his 35th year; then gave it up after reading a scare book on the subject. Within a few weeks, compulsive ideas about killing his wife.

A professor; masturbated daily up to the age of forty; in fairly good health; gave up the habit; after a few months, dizziness, agoraphobia, inability to eat and other neurotic symptoms.

A fact that may be corroborated every time: the neurosis breaks out only after the subjects give up the habit of masturbation. The disease is afterwards falsely regarded as a consequence of the habit instead of being properly recognized as due to abstinence from masturbation. Any one taking the trouble to look into the anamneses of serious neuroses will find frequently enough that the patients give up masturbation and that the respective trouble developed only subsequently. In my work, *Morbid Anxiety States and their Treatment* (Authorized English version by *Dr. James S. Van*

Teslaar), I have recorded a large number of illustrative cases.

On the other hand, I know persons who have been addicted to the habit for years without showing a trace of any ill effect. A man, 54 years of age, has confessed to me that he has masturbated daily since his early childhood; frequently a number of times through a single day. He is married and, besides masturbating, he has daily intercourse with his wife. His potentia is excellent and he shows no signs of so-called neurasthenic stigmata.

Another case from my professional observation is that of an artist who has masturbated regularly from his fourth to his sixteenth year. After that, daily pollutions nearly drove him to despair, until a physician advised him to overcome the pollutions by indulging freely in sexual intercourse. So long as he had intercourse but once a week this did not help. But when he was fortunate enough to find a sweetheart who made strong demands upon him, his pollutions disappeared, never to return. This man shows no ill effect in body or mind and he has achieved a high rung upon the ladder of social position. Neither has his potentia suffered, so that it has given him the reputation of being quite a Don Juan.

Next I want to draw attention to the history of a 41-year-old lawyer, whose case I have partly recorded in the *Zentrablatt f. Psychoanalyse* (vol. III, p. 250):

CASE 9. "I suffer from abnormal sexual desire, which I gratify through masturbation. At 16 years of age a colleague masturbated before me. A few weeks later, I saw a gentleman gracefully kissing a lady's hand and the scene evoked in me a pleasurable sensation such as I had not felt theretofore. At night in bed I reproduced in my phantasy the scene I had witnessed; I recalled also my colleague in the act of masturbating and indulged for the first time. Since that occurrence I have masturbated daily, later more often, occasionally as often as six times in a day. The accompanying phantasy was always a hand kiss which either I or some one else bestowed on a lady. If I saw some one kissing a lady's hand, or if I myself had an opportunity to do so, or even if I had only read about such a scene, or saw it portrayed, it roused immense libido in me and I had to seek gratification at once through masturbation. The greater the devotion or humility displayed in the hand kiss the stronger my libido. Since I always had the opportunity of witnessing hand kisses, or of kissing ladies' hands, my sexual excitation was continual and I always had to seek release through masturbation. When I learned during my University years that my sexual sensitiveness was something abnormal and that the form of gratification in

which I practiced was harmful, the perverse trouble
was already so deeply rooted that it was useless to
fight against it. In spite of the most earnest resolutions the lightest incitation again drew me back into
the habit. This also prevented me from finishing
my study course in time, because while preparing for
the final examinations, the necessary isolation caused
me to indulge inordinately in the habit. Instead of
studying I gave myself up to my erotic phantasies.
Twice I attempted coitus, without success. The
puella did rouse me. As the erection proceeded but
slowly, the *puella*, impatiently, began to taunt me,
and that broke the charm. A beautiful woman is
capable of rousing me through and for herself, so
that I have the feeling that under the proper cicum-
stances I could gratify my sexual impulse in a normal way.

So far as I know there have been no mental or
sexual abnormalities in my family.

As a physical consequence I can mention only a
certain lassitude and often a drawing in the limbs,
especially in the feet. Mentally I am normal,
possessing a rather keen wit and, as the leader of a
busy law office, I may state that I display an energetic spirit."

Thus, the masturbator's report of himself. He
confesses to me that *during the past ten years he has
never masturbated less than three times a day.*

And what about the man's appearance? We have

before us a flourishing, well nourished man, without
any grey hair; normal muscular power; reflexes
slightly increased; otherwise nothing abnormal.

In short, a typical masturbation case of 25 years'
duration (of the type called *Onanismus*, and considered pathologic), but without a trace of neurasthenia, such as *Freud* [3] considers typical of the inveterate practice of this habit. No pressure around
the head, no fatigue (only some degree of weariness), no dyspepsia, no constipation, and no spinal
irritation.

Weariness and ache in the limbs are symptoms
that do not make up a "disease." The ache is distinctly rheumatic. It is not necessary to go into
the psychology of this case. The libido, obviously,
depends on a feeling of submissiveness towards
women, a feeling which probably covers his real weakness. The episode about the prostitute shows that
while his attitude is one of submissiveness so far as
his phantasies are concerned, in reality he cannot
endure being humbled. But the case is recommended
to the attention of all sexologists who still hold to
the belief that masturbation is harmful. I refer
them also to another case, mentioned in the Discussions (*vid.* prev. foot-note, for reference): a man in
the late forties, masturbating daily, and also having

[3] *Die Sexualät in der Ætiologie der Neurosen.* Sammlung
kleiner Schriften zur Neurosenlehre. 1906. Vol. I.

daily intercourse with his wife, yet in full possession
of his potentia, a fact corroborated by the testimony of his wife, in whom he induces several times
orgasms during a single congressus sexualis.

I know very many men and women, who have abandoned themselves to the habit with the intention of
doing away with themselves in that pleasant manner. Even *Goethe* has confessed that in Leipzig he
had likewise given himself over to his "physical
nature." I know, for instance, a woman who for a
long period has masturbated as many as six times
in the course of each night. She had read of Japa-
nese women exciting their sexual parts by the introduction of silver balls set to vibrate and she has
procured for herself a vibrator, under the pretext
of needing it for her pains. She uses the vibrator to
rouse the clitoris, occasionally also for internal irritation, and thus she attains extraordinary orgasm.
During the period of her addiction to masturbation,
a veritable onanistic spree, her health bloomed forth
and she gained about twenty lbs. in weight. Only
after the fight against the vibrator, she began to
develop a neurosis, but that disappeared as soon as
she resumed the habit. She wanted me to tell her
whether she would really bring on some spinal
trouble if she did not give up the practice. She
resisted the attempt at studying analytically her
sexual life. There were things she would not dis-

close to a soul on earth! After a few years I met her incidentally on the street. She looked well and claimed to be in excellent health. She would not disclose anything about her subsequent mode of gratification.

Es gibt nur eine Art Liebe, aber tausend verschiedene Nachahmungen.

                                   LA ROCHEFOUCAULD

III

Pollution as a Form of Onanism—Case of *Follen
Cabot*—Case from Personal Observation—A Woman
who suffers from Pollutions—The Struggle against
Pollutions—Sleeplessness and Headache—A Student
complaining of 4-5 Nightly Pollutions—Search for
the Specific Phantasy—Onanism during the Hysteric
Attack—Alleged Dangers of Onanism induced by a
Guilty Conscience—Sweet Fainting—Excitation of
Erogenous Zones—Prolongation of Fore-Pleasure at
Expense of End-Pleasure—Cryptic Orgasm—Der-
matoses as Substitutes for Onanism—Pruritus Vul-
vae—Spermatorrhœa—Anal   Eroticism — Luther's
Illness—Day Dreams with Psychic Onanism—Case
of Compulsion Neurosis following the Abandonment
of the Habit; Recovery after Habit was Resumed—
Ungratified Persons become Criminals.

III

Love is one, though there are numberless imitations.

LA ROCHEFOUCAULD

Strife and play are the constituents of human life. Both strife and play instincts are directed inwardly in neurosis. The neurotic struggles and plays with self (*i.e.*, he *poses* before self).

In masturbation, too, the instinct of self-gratification manifests itself as a form of struggle as well as a form of play. We now turn our attention particularly to the forms which display the conflict as a game. There are numberless persons who take pride in having very easily overcome the masturbation habit. That many persons should have been able to give up the habit easily is due to two factors: In the first place the masturbation act was a matter of convenience for them, something they could easily detach from the sexual act proper. The specific accompanying phantasy was the sexual act itself, without complications, without paraphilia, with no other complicating or unrealizable accompaniments. In the second place, moreover, these persons continue to masturbate in their sleep. This form of

107

masturbation is called pollution.[1a] But many persons are wholly unaware of the pollution and then proudly proclaim their ability to live abstinently for a long time. We shall presently reveal a whole series of such cryptic forms of onanism. According to my observations these are even more common than ordinary masturbation.[1] I quote, after *Rohleder*, a very characteristic case reported by *Folen Cabot*.

CASE 10. A student, 22 years of age, physically and mentally in good health and also sexually normal, dreamed that he may masturbate without danger to his health, in fact, that this form of sexual gratification was the best for him. He woke up *post ejaculationem*, greatly depressed and disgusted with himself. The consequence was loss of self-confidence and fear of mental disease. All therapeutic measures, bromides, regulation of the diet and of the activities, both physical and mental, even prophylactic binding of the hands, and the bandaging of the genitalia, proved useless. Leather gloves (locked together at the wrist) were removed at night, the patient during his sleep finding the key hidden in a vessel, while in a somnambulistic state. After waking up, complete amnesia. Recovery through marriage. . . .

[1] *Rohleder* estimates one unconscious masturbator among one hundred.
[1a] Emission of semen at other times than in coition. Pollution is used here synonymously with emission. (*Ed. note.*)

How unlike the older generations. They would have interpreted the dream as a divine command just as nowadays the mentally deranged frequently find themselves ordered to practice masturbation. They refer to divine voices commanding them to masturbate. I have once treated an exhilarated student, who after some hesitation confessed to me that he has discovered the one infallible means for prolonging life, perhaps for attaining immortality. It was masturbation; and he was not a little surprised to hear that this practice was considered harmful by many physicians, when an inner voice told him the contrary. Such cases of masturbation during sleep and in dreams as the one mentioned above I have had frequent opportunity to observe. I have quoted the above case, only to show how barbarously the sexual instinct is still being mistreated in modern times. The recovery through marriage shows that this was merely an instance of *Notoanie* (convenience habit) and that the young man lacked only a proper outlet. Instead of that he was given a pair of leather gloves and wrist locks,—reminders of darkest middle ages.

The very next case shows us a man who very properly conceived his pollutions to be an "unconscious masturbation."

CASE 11. A patient writes me as follows:

Dear Doctor:

I shall make an attempt to describe to you my
present state as well as the origin of my trouble.

I am now 23 years of age. I was a very lively
and gifted fellow during my earlier school years,
though I suffered even then from periodic headaches
and bed-wetting; but otherwise I had no serious
illness.

At 13 years of age I was taught by my school
comrades to masturbate, I indulged in the practice
daily, always thinking of regular intercourse; but
later my phantasies changed and I masturbated with
feelings of anxiety.

Every school task inspired me with the fear of not
getting through in time; this would at once plunge
me into anxiety, a state that would rapidly grow
worse, ending in ejaculation, although there was no
complete erection.

At first I did not worry much about it, practicing
the habit perhaps once daily, and I was otherwise
fairly comfortable. But later there fell into my
hands a book, giving a lurid account of the evils
of masturbation. From that time on I always experienced a terrific mental struggle before yielding.
Each time I solemnly promised myself never to do
it again, but all my resolutions did me no good, I
always yielded again. The result was again a severe
depression.

These struggles never ceased. I grew sad, became
retired in disposition, distracted, forgetful, unable
to keep up my studies, and during my later high
school years I needed tutoring, although during the

first couple of high school grades I had been a model scholar.

During the sixth high school year I fell in love with my new landlord's 14-year old daughter. It was my first love affair and the love was reciprocated. A purely platonic affair. I have never had erections in the presence of the girl, although we were frequently together for long periods and we indulged freely in endearments and kisses. This ideal friendship lasted that way about a year; it freed me of the worry and restlesness due to my habit and it also enabled me to fight it more successfully. I was even able to abstain from masturbating for a week or two at a stretch and I was content. But presently I became aware of the pollutions which had remained unobserved theretofore. *I regarded them as a form of unconscious masturbation* and then I thought that there was no salvation possible for me inasmuch as the pollutions had started in as soon as I gave up masturbating and I had read that pollutions also lead to insanity and impotence; I preferred deliberately to masturbate rather than to be subject to the involuntary pollutions.

Eventually I attempted sexual intercourse with a peasant girl and I failed on account of incomplete erection. Consequently I thought I was impotent and, as a last resort, I consulted a specialist; the latter advised me to enter his sanitarium, holding out the promise of a complete cure; but partly for financial reasons, and partly because I feared that my trouble would become known among all my acquaintances, I found myself unable to accept the advice.

I gave up every hope of a cure, changed my

boarding house in order to be no longer near the girl that reminded me constantly of my unattainable happiness.

I avoided all social intercourse, felt myself hopelessly lost, and had frequent thoughts of suicide.

The simplest school task now became irksome to me, my memory failed me and it was with great difficulty that I pulled through high school.

After the final examinations I set for myself another ideal. I decided to renounce all worldly pleasures and to devote myself entirely to the pursuit of science.

During my first University year I lived like an automaton, communicated with no one, and kept to my studies, so that at the end of the second semester I passed with flying colors the first three examinations. But this success brought me neither peace nor happiness. I am still depressed and unhappy, especially when I see my colleagues so happy and care free.

My life is a continual torture, the least provocation brings on great anxiety, my heart flutters and I am a sick man. My memory is very weak and I find no real enjoyment in anything I do. I hardly dare hope for a cure because I fear that my trouble is too advanced; nevertheless, I beg you, dear doctor, to relieve me of this physical and mental torture, if it be at all possible. . . .

G. H. (Med. Student).

This case illustrates the well known form of masturbation which is governed by affects. The subject masturbates with anxiety. We see further that the fear of masturbation bringing on impotence, renders the young man impotent. The gruesome fear of insanity also lurks in the background. We note further the frequently emphasized tendency to asceticism; the subject wants to renounce all worldly pleasures and to devote himself exclusively to the pursuit of science. Masturbation accompanied by anxiety holds out no hopeful prospect of being transposed into heterosexual uses because in the presence of woman as a sexual partner the subject will always conjure up fear and will react with *ejaculatio praecox*, unless psychoanalytic treatment brings about a "*redressement psychique*," *i. e.*, a psychic readjustment.

The insight into the nature of his pollution reflects credit upon the medical student, many experienced "*finished*" practitioners are at a loss to understand it.

The next case takes us much more deeply into the heart of our problem:

CASE 12.   During last Summer a woman consulted me for sleeplessness. Her insomnia was of the kind frequently observed in anxiety neurosis. The patient falls asleep easily, but wakes up with a start, her heart beats fast, she experiences a tremendous feeling of dread and tosses in bed for hours without being able to fall asleep again. All sorts of queer thoughts go through her mind but she is unable to recall them. The trouble was probably brought on by masturbation, a habit which she has practiced since childhood, up to a few months ago. She has found out from physicians' talks and through reading that by her indulgence she has completely ruined her nervous system. For this she reproaches herself most ruefully. Her husband knows nothing about her sleeplessness; she is afraid to confess her trouble to him, lest he think: aha! —she has masturbated again. Her insomnia is now aggravated by a torturing remorse. She is thinking all the time: how happy she might be had she never masturbated! In her mind hover most bitter reproaches against her mother who should have advised her and who might have saved her from falling into the habit. She struggles with suicidal ideas feeling that she cannot endure life any longer unless I can make her sleep.

The case is typical. Our patient was well so long as she masturbated. Within a few weeks after her self-enforced abstinence her insomnia began and shortly thereafter her thoughts of self-reproach. We find over and over this to be the case. Our patient also harbors thoughts of suicide. An important law holds true of our mental life, the *lex talionis,* the eye-for-an-eye law of compensation. No one thinks of self-destruction who does not harbor thoughts of murder against some other person. From that standpoint our case requires further light.

The following facts bring the required additional light in the case under consideration: I explain to the woman the utterly harmless character of the masturbation habit to which she has been addicted in so mild a form. But in the face of her great feeling of self-reproach the explanation is useless. Her sleeplessness is not abated thereby nor is her feeling of self-reproach diminished. Her regrets and reproaches are endless. I am compelled to investigate the deeper psychic forces of her neurosis and here is what I find out: Two years previously the woman has experienced a great shock. She is married to a man ten years older than herself, whose *potentia sexualis* is rather weak. After coitus she was compelled to resort to masturbation in order to attain her orgasm. The man indulged in his marital duties less frequently as time went on, as an excuse pointing to his neurasthenia, which forbade him frequent sexual intercourse. There are intervals of several months. One day the servant girl gave her notice of leave because she could not stand it any longer in the house, the "gentleman of the house," would not leave her alone. For months he had been pursuing her and to protect herself she must leave.

This information naturally led to unpleasant quarrel scenes. She wanted a separation and denied the penitent man any signs of forgiveness. What particularly troubled her was her own "missed" past. She had been a beautiful, attractive woman, very many men had been after her, and she had had endless opportunities of yielding to temptation. Her first thought was to revenge herself. But she was already the mother of grown up children. And could she begin, at 40 years of age, living a fast life, after having followed strictly the straight and narrow path till now? Ah!—why had she been so foolish? If she only had the power to live over her past and make up for lost opportunities. The thought of revenge grew in her mind. But her husband, now mistrusting her and jealous, tried to catch her in compromising situations so as to be even with her. On her part, she could not turn downright "bad," even though she might think of it. She had been brought up too strictly for that. So long as the husband lived she did not want to deceive him. That was the thought which came to her mind once when her husband returned home with a fever. And shortly thereafter the reflection came to her: if your husband should now die, you would be free to do as you please! But her husband recovered and the household became more annoying to her than ever. Soon other relief-yielding thoughts came to her mind, leading to fancies of poisoning, all inspired alike by the desire for revenge. These fancies were for the most part unconscious. Now the psychic conflict seemed practically insolvable, inasmuch as the patient was not conscious of some of these incitations and motives.

And it was only at that juncture that she ceased to masturbate. As a matter of fact she had never experienced any pleasure in coitus. She was psychically anesthetic so that the practice of masturbation by the friction of the clitoris always meant more to her than sexual intercourse. But suddenly the thought came to her that she has ruined herself through the masturbation habit and she became a victim of the most severe self-reproaches. We note that, as a matter of fact, these self-reproaches had been transposed. They originated elsewhere. Masturbation is the bearer of all feelings of guilt. The habit is charged up with all the feelings of remorse which originate anywhere, so long as those feelings cannot or must not become conscious. Masturbation is the representative of all guilt.

That was the case in the present instance. The woman reproached herself for her death-wishes against her husband and for her other criminal thoughts. These affects were transposed over to the masturbation habit. Only now may we understand her suicidal impulses! These were a punishment for her thoughts of poisoning. The giving up of masturbation was also decreed by the inner judge. She adjudged herself guilty and punished herself by abstaining from the highest physical pleasure she knew, masturbation. But, on the other hand, she was unable to endure life without indulging in the habit. . . . She was sleepless because insufficient sexual gratification is the chief cause of sleeplessness, as I have explained at length in my *Nervous Anxiety States.*[2]

Her insomnia was of a peculiar type: she first fell quietly asleep only to wake up with a sense of great dread in the midst of gruesome dreams. What was she dreaming about? She told me some of the dreams. They were about love affairs with strange men. Just before or during the orgasms she woke up with a jerk and always found her hand in contact with the genitalia. Thus she continued to masturbate in her sleep.

This case also illustrates the most common form of unconscious masturbation: pollutions. All neurotics follow a significant principle and unless we are aware of that, many of their symtomatic outbreaks seem unexplainable. The principle may be called: *Lust ohne Schuld*, pleasure without guilt. Pollution is a form of masturbation for which one is not responsible. The reproaches can no longer be directed against self. But our patient assumed also responsibility for her dreams. Even in the dream she did not want to sin, she did not want to indulge in a sinful orgasm. She wanted to remain a chaste woman. That was the secret punishment

[2] Trsl. by *James S. Van Teslaar.*

which she had unconsciously imposed upon herself. Therefore she dreaded the nights, her dread being really traceable to her evil nightly thoughts or phantasies. She could not fall asleep because she had to watch herself, so as to be sure not to masturbate during sleep.

I am now recording the end of the case. Bringing up the criminal fancies of doing away with the husband and the patient's candid clearing up of her thoughts had a fairly gratifying result. The patient slept for five hours at a stretch with the aid of one-half gr. *Adalin*. But she woke up in the night and fearing that she could not fall asleep again, took another half gram, etc. Of course a patient is not cured so long as she has to take a drug and so long as she is not free of her nightly dreads. The nocturnal anxiety clung to her. But one day she came to me beaming delight. She had slept peacefully throughout the previous night. She was cured. Weeks later she told me that she began sleeping properly only after she resumed the habit of masturbating. Her very appearance changed very markedly. She was once more happy, could laugh and take pleasure in things,—briefly she felt as a person in good health should and she was well.

In a case of this kind where are the alleged dangers of masturbation? We may confidently conclude that in such a case the practice is a necessity without the fear of being called "advocates" of masturbation. In my judgment the masturbation advocates, so-called, have positively caused less harm than the "secret vice" hounds. . . . But the case shows us also that the feeling of guilt associated with the masturbation habit raises a very complicated problem. We witness here a stubborn struggle against unconscious onanism as the result of self-punishment.

Any unprejudiced observer meets instances of this kind. I know compulsion neurotics who became well, gained weight and assumed healthy activities as soon as they were permitted a certain measure of self-gratification. All psycho-therapeutists will agree with me that the most severe types of neuroses are found among those who are apparently abstinent or who have never masturbated.

I have stated at the outset that everybody masturbates. The alleged "abstinent" persons must have also masturbated. And usually they have done so to an excessive extent. They do not know it, that they do not even suspect it, only shows the depths of their repression, it indicates the split of their psyche, it shows us the wide cleft that exists between their consciousness and the unconscious. Such cases are severe and difficult to treat because a great deal of trouble is required to ferret out and render conscious their infantile and cryptic forms of onanistic indulgence. All persons apparently abstinent indulge in some form or other of cryptic (larvated), unconscious masturbation.

The most common form, as already mentioned, is pollution. Many persons assume a very strict attitude against pollution and carry on a very bitter struggle against the habit. The healthy minded person accepts the occurrence of pollution as a fact and in some cases actually regards it as a welcome relief. Having found in this form of onanism an indulgence without the participation of consciousness, *i. e.* without personal guilt, he enjoys the harmless self-deception. The neurotic whose indulgence in masturbation is accompanied by phantasies which always dip into the forbidden struggles against the habit because it is linked with incest fancies, criminal trends, or paraphilias. He tries to overcome the pollutions by means of a strict diet, hard bed, drugs, physical exercise to the point of exhaustion, hypnosis, etc. Every pollution inspires him with fears for his health and worst feelings of dread. Usually the pollutions set in when the young men are scared into giving up the masturbation habit by reading the books or attending the lectures of professional "purity" crusaders. When they start masturbating again the pollutions disappear. We know already: normal sexual intercourse does not always cure pollutions. In some case the pollutions cease entirely when the men turn to regular sexual intercourse and indulge often enough. But others may indulge in intercourse and soon thereafter have pollutions or must masturbate. Why is that?

It is because these men do not find intercourse with woman a form of sexual gratification adequate for their needs, or because in the act of sexual intercourse only a portion of their erotism is satisfied, while other components of their erotism, like all hungry instincts, still crave fulfillment. There are cryptic homosexuals, persons who themselves are unaware of their homosexual trends, and persons of this type always masturbate after intercourse with a woman.

The various forms of pollution are nothing but a more or less adroitly hidden masturbation. Many patients admit that fact openly. They themselves are surprised to find their hands handling the genitalia during sleep, though they try to avoid doing so and adopt all sorts of manipulations and devices in the attempt to secure their hands outside their bed covers.

Indeed, the struggle against pollutions may be as bitter as the fight against masturbation proper. I know many persons who suffer from sleeplessness [3] because they are afraid of pollutions and of the accompanying inciting dreams. Often the inciting dream is forgotten. A "dull headache" in the morning, or a heavy pressure over the head (the well

[3] *Cp. Stekel, The Will to Sleep;* A Lecture. Verlag, Bergmann, Wiesbaden, 1915.

known iron-band-around-the head, for a long time regarded as a sign of so-called "neurasthenia") disclose to the experienced psychotherapeutist that the subjects, on awakening, have made strong efforts to forget, *i. e.* repress, their nocturnal dream.

Young men are badly scared particularly by the occurrence of repeated pollutions. These are veritable orgies of the unconscious, carried on by means of the entangling and kaleidoscopic dream pictures. The feeling of guilt roused by the dream pictures is enhanced by the accompanying hypochrondriac notions. The badly scared pollutionists imagine that their health is hopelessly ruined, they fear that they will never get well, that they will suffer from spinal cord disease or that they will become insane. They rush tremblingly from one specialist to another, begging help. But all internal medications (bromides, camphor, lupulin), and all dietetic prescriptions prove useless; and even psychotherapy may fail if the patients have not the courage of meeting their problem with candor.

Occasionally it is possible to quiet the alarmed patient and by a friendly talk, advice, or explanations, to bring peace into his life, or to "cure" him. In the case which I am about to record, this, unfortunately, was not found possible. The next case is significant also because the patient himself soon perceived that the pollutions were but a form of masturbation. This view of the matter he had not

derived from me. He himself came to it.   Among
patients who consult us for pollutions there are
always a number to whom the expression pollutions is an euphemism for masturbation. That is
how they confess the habit to the physician.
Elderly men, in particular, are ashamed to confess
that they feel impelled to masturbate and complain
instead of pollutions alleged to occur at night,
against their will.

CASE 13. Mr. Alpha complains that he has 4-5
pollutions every night. He is 25 years of age
and claims never to have masturbated. The pollutions occur as follows: he wakes up at night and
finds himself tremendously excited. No erection, the
membrum virile but partly stiff. He turns to one
side and as soon as the membrum touches the thigh,
ejaculation.

He shows signs of a beginning Basedow's: emacia-
tion, exophthalmos, rapid pulse, profuse perspira-
tion, occasional diarrhœa. No struma. Unable to
account for the sudden pollutions. For about two
years has maintained relations with a woman—but
about two months ago has given up the affair without any apparent reason. Has tried to overcome
the pollutions through regular sexual intercourse.
No orgasm. Except once. That was when he had
intercourse with his friend's sweetheart. Tremendous orgasm, strong erection, great potence. In

spite of that, four pollutions during the same night.

At the next visit states that the pollutions are, strictly speaking, masturbation. He is quasi-unconscious at the time, as in a trance, and knows not what he is doing. On the morning following the pollutions (or, more strictly speaking, after the masturbation, for he actually handles his privates), he feels all broken up and unable to carry on any task requiring mental application. Plagues himself with suicidal thoughts. Afraid of insanity. Prescribed 3 grams Sedobrol, at night. Refuses psychoanalysis; advise him to enter a sanitarium. This advice he also turns down claiming lack of means do not permit him to accept it. (Subsequently it turns out that he did not want to go to a sanitarium.)

The condition persists in spite of Sedobrol. Masturbates "innumerable" times. Unable to tell exactly how many times. Finally I discover that the pollutions set in since sharing sleeping quarters with brother and a friend. I advise him to sleep in a room of his own giving as reason that he must have fresh air.

Has not followed the advice. He cannot stay in a room without the brother. He fears he will die. He must not be alone. He accuses the brother of being responsible for his trouble. The brother is the one who dissuades him from normal sexual intercourse claiming that it is weakening. His brother is against any intercourse with women. *It is becoming clearer all along that he masturbates with homosexual phantasies.* The subject is unaware of the phantasies accompanying his masturbation. He does not want to know what he thinks of during masturbation and claims: nothing at all!

Attempts again to turn his libido upon a woman; the result: no orgasm. Erection persists for hours, but there follows no ejaculation, although this occurs very promptly if he touches the *membrum* with his own hand. He still fights very persistently against my suggestion of sleeping in a room of his own and stubbornly rejects also the idea of sanitarium treatment. Could not the brother sleep in an adjoining room? He mentions his illness, his weakness, his anxiety as reasons why he cannot be alone. He confesses that he has masturbated in spite of the girl's presence.

"What are you thinking about when you masturbate?"

"I do not know."

"You do not want to know."

"You are right. I do not care to know it. There come to me foolish thoughts. I shall never tell them. . . ."

"Why not?"

"Because I am ashamed. But perhaps I may give you some idea. It is an episode from childhood. Something foolish, the carryings on of children, you know. It is foolish things like that I think of, always. Tell me, is there no relief from such foolish notions? Why do they pursue me day and night? I always fall asleep alright, then around half-past twelve or one o'clock I awake and the pollutions begin. I awake with pollution."

"You mean, you masturbate. . . ."

"I cannot help it. I do."

Two days later I am told that he has shot himself. A contribution to the problem: masturbation and suicide! He carried the secret of his trouble to his grave. We may presume that he fought with all his strength against homosexual phantasies. Women had lost all charm for him. Brother and the friend were his only associates. He took complete possession of them and prevented them from giving any attention to others. During the last two months he experienced orgasm but once and that was when he had intercourse with his friend's sweetheart. The significance of this is fully pointed out in my study of homosexuality.[4]

The friend's sweetheart was the means whereby he could attain possession of the friend, a "mask for homosexuality." After he found out that other women could not rouse orgasm in him, he became sad and depressed. No woman was able to substitute

---

[4] *Cp. Stekel, Bi-Sexual Love*, also, *The Homosexual Neurosis*, authorized English version by *James S. Van Teslaar*, Badger, Gorham Press, Boston, 1922.

for him the orgasm of masturbation.   But he did not want to masturbate any longer and rather than admit his homosexual phantasies he preferred to give up life.   Before his mental vision the break of these phantasies into consciousness was an ever threatening danger.   The danger pursued him so that his poor mind became a whirl and he dreaded insanity.   That fear drove him to take his life.   He committed suicide in the house of his beloved brother's house.   He withdrew to the water closet when his brother refused him a trivial request and shot himself through the head.

The specific phantasies accompanying the dreams responsible for the pollutions are of the greatest significance.   (Additional examples will illustrate this further, and the chapters which follow will also bring additional support to our present contentions.)   If we inquire after the pollution dream we often hear that the patient has forgotten it or that he had not observed clearly the face of the love objective in the dream.   Others express their surprise at the numerous paraphilias portrayed in the dream and facetiously remark that such doings are so far from their mind, "they wouldn't dream of it."

These facts are also of greatest significance when we consider the rational therapy of pollutions.   We must often investigate the conditions surrounding the patients and under which they live.   The most remarkable cures may be accomplished by a simple

measure, such as a change in the environment. It
sometimes happens that subjects suffer from pollutions in one locality but are entirely free in some
other locality. They ascribe this to the change of
air. But it depends on the associations linked to
the respective localities,—it is a matter of environmental influence.

Thus, for instance, I had advised the above patient
to leave Vienna. I am convinced that his condition
would have improved in the midst of other surround-
ings, that a stay at a sanitarium would have saved
the promising life of that highly gifted young man.

Another form of unconscious onanism is masturbation during hysterical seizures which occur in all
possible gradations, from the major hysteric attacks with the arc-de-cercle down to the occasional
slight "absences" lasting but a few seconds. All
states involving the suppression of consciousness in-
volve also the carrying out of forbidden deeds. One
of these, specifically the most common, is masturbation. The indulgence is associated with various
phantasies, including criminal and perverse notions.[5]
If any of these phantasies threaten to break into
consciousness, the onanistic act is carried out unconsciously during the hysterical attack. The characteristic movements seen in certain hysterical seiz-

[5] *Cp.* my study, *Die psychische Behandlung der Epilepsie*
(The Psychic Treatment of E.), Ztrbl. f. Psychoanalyse, vol.
I; also, *Stekel, Nervous Anxiety States,* trsl. *Van Teslaar.*

ures leave no doubt as to that and plain masturbation, bed wetting, or seminal loss are also to be observed. After the attack these patients experience either a deep feeling of guilt, a sense of torturing remorse, or else they state that they feel themselves very much eased (as if without weight, as if having wings). Similar states may be observed after sexual intercourse or after masturbatory acts. The old Latin saying, *post coitum omne animal triste* is decidedly false. The mood following the deed depends on whether the deed is associated or not with a feeling of guilt.

The alleged harm of masturbation is a problem to be solved only in that light. A person who masturbates without a sense of guilt (without anxiety), feels no harm after temperate indulgence, and suffers no harmful consequences. All contrary observations are due to the misunderstanding of a psychogenetic depression. If the masturbator thinks he has harmed himself, if he is filled with false teachings, his sense of guilt will conjure up after every indulgence all the symptoms ascribed to masturbation. *I have never yet found any evil consequences among persons who did not believe the practice to be harmful.* All the harm is generated through autosuggestion by the feelings of anxiety. Many practitioners are still unaware that anxiety, or fear, is responsible for some of the most serious ailments. I have known a physician who, having gone through syphilis, had acquired a hysterical pseudo-tabes on account of his fear of tabes.

We return to our problem, the larvated forms of onanism. There are women who turn suddenly ill, they feel weak and merge into a sweet swoon.[6] Such fainting spells represent the orgasm after an unconscious or half-conscious onanistic act as the sewing machine, or accompanying a phantasy (psychic onanism), after an automatic game, etc. These symbolic forms of masturbation are very frequent. They include nose boring, certain finger movements, pocket games, handling the various body openings, etc.

In such cases either the phantasy is excited or some erogenous zone is roused. The erogenous zone may be either the skin or the mucous membrane, and any portion of the body may be involved. I have by no means gone over exhaustively the available forms of larvated onanism. That would be almost impossible. I want merely to point out that there are forms of indulgence which the masturbator himself does not recognize or acknowledge as masturbation. I know a woman who masturbates by means of *immissio et frictio digitis in anum*. She knows she masturbates and achieves complete orgasm in that manner. That is avowedly masturbation. But another woman claims she must dis-

[6] *Stekel, Nervous Anxiety States,* unabridged English version by *Van Teslaar.*

tend her anus,—a procedure both very painful and
unpleasant to her,—otherwise her bowels would not
move.   Before every bowel movement she must dis-
tend her anus.   That is larvated (cryptic, or hidden) masturbation.   But how does it happen that
the orgasm does not bring to her mind the true
character of her procedure?   Or may the orgasm
be wholly left out?

All such cases of masked onanism experience a
form of orgasm.   But there is a tendency to weaken
that orgasm and to hide it entirely from consciousness.   *In most cases of unconscious masturbation*
the fore-pleasure is greatly prolonged, or parcelled
out over a greater period and its libidinous char-
acter is thus masked, while the end-pleasure is sub-
dued, if not left out altogether, so that it is per-
ceived in consciousness not as gratification, but as
weakness, fatigue or fainting.

Indeed the gratification feature of the experience
may be glossed over entirely by the prominence of
apparent pains.   The painful cramps of problematic origin are of this type.   Such mystifying painful cramps may be observed particularly in children.
Parents are badly scared over the occurrence.
But the experienced physician observes quite a disparity between the alleged pains and the note of
contentment more or less plainly depicted in the
child's face and should have no difficulty in diagnos-
ing the condition as larvated masturbation.   Such

masked orgasm may be achieved also by some other path than the auto-erotic. I know a woman who took massage treatments for a number of months on account of uterine prolapse. The massaging was done by a lay person and after each massage, which proved harmful in every way, the woman suffered from nausea, disgust for food and a number of other nervous symptoms, including remarkable cramps, during which all the patient's limbs were stiff. In connection with these cramp attacks she complained also of shivering and strong gastric pains. As the spell ended, her pale face turned red, and she fell into a comfortable state of relaxation and sleepiness.

The cramps were an unconscious repetition of the massaging. The stiffness of the limbs corresponded to the muscular tension at the height of the orgasm, a condition analogous to the well known arc-de-cercle of hysteria and of women suffering from erotomania.

I know fencers who masturbate with the aid of their muscles. They induce great tension in all the muscles of their body and thus achieve orgasm. Many forms of cryptic onanism take place the same way.[7]

All such persons are apparently unaware of having experienced an orgasm. On the contrary, they

[7] *Cp.* the very instructive essay by *Ernst Marcus*, already mentioned, *Ueber verschiedene Formen der Lustgewinnung am eigenen Leibe* (Various Forms of Pleasurable Gratification on one's own Body), Ztrbl. f. Psychoanalyse, vol. III, No. 3.

complain of pains. Thus the woman mentioned above, who was taking massage treatments, insisted that the ordeal was a torture to her, and that she would be happy to be through with the treatment. But she continued going to the masseur and protested most vigorously when her husband, noticing the remarkable change it induced in her, tried to have her give up the treatment. Her argument was that one must carry out a plan of treatment to the end, once one had begun it, as well as put up with the "little unpleasantnesses." She did not want to give up her orgasm. Had one tried to explain to her the character of her pains, the woman would have indignantly protested. Persons are rarely willing to recognize that they continue masturbating in hidden, round-about ways. These forms of indulgence serve to quiet one's conscience, they are means for avoiding the self-reproaches connected with direct auto-erotic indulgence.

The forms of a larvated onanism which manifest themselves as dermal itching are even more common. For instance, a 70-year old woman suffers from *pruritus vulvae* and cannot fall asleep, unless she first thoroughly scratches the respective parts. The scratching replaces masturbation and is kept up until a mitigated orgasm is thereby produced. A 50-year old woman finds her body itching all over, before bed time; her husband, daughter, son, the whole family must help scratch her skin. Towards the last the woman herself does the scratching, wherever the itching is at its worst, as mentioned, until she suddenly feels a strong desire to urinate; that seems to end the ordeal; and after that she is able to fall asleep. The scene repeats itself every evening. Many problematic cases of urticaria and other neuro-dermatoses proving refractory to every form of treatment and ushered in with intensive itching are but cryptic forms of masturbation.

A common form of masturbation, spermatorrhœa, or seminal losses, I have already mentioned as a typical complaint of sexually abstinent males. Among men who indulge frequently in sexual intercourse I have never found this complaint. The seminal loss in question occurs sometimes with a slight, or perhaps even with a fairly marked pleasurable feeling. Such pleasurable feelings may also accompany emptying of the bowels, disclosing that the anus is an erogenous zone. Indeed, it is erroneous to think that masturbation involves only the genital organs proper. Any erogenous zone may serve as a center for the indulgence. The anus is an erogenous zone of first order. For that reason this region is the center of endless varieties of cryptic masturbation. Some subjects bore into the rectum with their finger, on account of itching, or because they think the fæcal masses must be dislodged, others because they want to push the protruding hæmorrhoids back into place, the woman

mentioned above because she thought she must en-
large the opening. Organic symptoms are always
seized upon to bring on the indispensable orgasm.

Many anal-erotics suffer from constipation. They
take advantage of their trouble and masturbate during their bowel movements. Young children are
already found to hold back their bowel contents because the passage of hardened fæces yields them
libido. For a similar reason sufferers from spermatorrhœa usually complain of constipation and
state that their seminal losses occur during their
bowel movements. That they experience a more or
less marked orgasm in connection with the occurrence is something these subjects admit but reluctantly.

Other anal-erotics play quite an exciting game
with the irrigator and after completely cleaning
out their bowels they feel refreshed, like born anew;
they admit that defæcation is the greatest pleasure
in their life. Their whole mental realm is pervaded
by anal-erotic imageries.

Likewise, hæmorrhoids, or anal fissures, which may
be very troublesome at times, are often induced
artificially, as the result of continual manipulations
around the anal region.

The irrigator is often but a means for pleasure
seeking, serving both men and women to excite the
respective parts under the guise of hygienic measures. For many persons the irrigator substitutes a

love objective so that I am not surprised to find that it plays a tremendous rôle in the phantasies of masturbators and fetichists.

Luther describes his anal troubles with great frankness. In a letter to *Melanchthon* he writes: "The Lord punished me with strong pains *in posterioribus;* my fæces are so hard I am compelled to move my bowels with great effort until the sweat breaks out; and the longer I postpone the ordeal, the harder the bowels. Yesterday my bowels moved again, after four days and that is why I have not been able to sleep the whole night and I am still restless. This trouble will be unbearable if it keeps up the way it has begun." The bowel trouble became so hopelessly bad that he wanted to give up all attempts at treatment. "Meanwhile," *Ebstein* relates in his study,[8] "the parts were kept raw and injured on account of the old manipulation, although he now used laxatives in profusion. In spite of the laxatives his local pains did not abate, either because the pills were drastic or for some other reason."

Such pains are substitutes for the libido. Of course that is not invariably the case, but it is true in many instances. *Luther's* constipation improved later on, but not his local pains. Occasionally he compared himself to the torn, injured, bleeding

[8] *Dr. Wilhelm Ebstein, Dr. Martin Luther's Krankheiten,* Ferdinand Enke, 1908.

woman in child bed. He calls his bleeding hæmorrhoids "*molimina excretoria.*" In addition to that
he suffered from stone and to this trouble he referred
saying that Satan was raging in him. Concerning his bleedings he wrote *Justus Jonas* in 1528:
"Such was my trouble that swelling appeared at
the opening when moving my bowels. There was
an itching sensation around it. This was the more
troublesome, the softer the bowels. If clotted blood
discharged I was better off and felt well, in fact
moving the bowels was pleasurable. The greater the
amount of clotted blood discharged, the greater was
my pleasurable sensation, so that this pleasant sensation induced me to move my bowels several times
daily. If I pressed with the finger against the swelling, blood would flow and there was a most agreeable itching sensation. Therefore in my judgment
this blood flow must not be at all stopped or diminished."

The libido connected with defæcation and the
pleasurable feel-sensations engendered by scratching
of the parts can hardly be pointed out more plainly.
Subsequently *Luther* suffered also from diarrœa and
tenesmus. The water closet is always very critical
place for him. In 1546 he underwent a crisis, on
account of his stone trouble, which fortunately
ended well; "a very big stone," which had endan-
gered his life, fell shortly after *Luther* had "at-
tended to his natural needs." Shortly thereafter

he had a phantasm: he saw the devil turn his posterior to his face.

Regarding *Luther's* early struggle with sexuality *Ebstein* relates: "Sexual excitations did not trouble him at first very much, but the more he protected himself the stronger he was roused by them. Nevertheless he preserved his chastity. He imposed all sorts of severe deprivations on himself through his excessive abstinence, at night he slept on bare boards with insufficient coverings, in warm weather he ran around almost naked, his body exposed to the sun's torturing rays. He grew thin and calls himself a drawn-and-dried fellow. While in this state of physical and mental exhaustion he once experienced some peculiar excitations and another time he showed eccentric changes in mood so that his associates at the monastery thought he was an epileptic, or possessed by demons.

I have mentioned the case of *Martin Luther* at some length because it discloses an excellent picture of anal-erotic peculiarities.

Of course, any other mucous surface lends itself to the development of similar peculiarities, especially the tongue. Various mannerisms of sucking, rolling the tongue, etc., belong to this category.

More common yet are the forms of larvated psychic onanism which are not associated with any manipulations. The subjects lose themselves in their dreams which end in ecstacies. They never know what they have been thinking about if they are called out of their day-dreams. Some minor symptomatic mannerisms may betray the content of their reveries. For instance, a man under my observation during his day dreams had the habit of seizing the *membrum* in hand, an occurrence about which he otherwise could tell nothing. He was a member of a Society for the Suppression of "lewd" Literature, a great Apostle of Purity, yet he spent half his waking life indulging in cryptic forms of masturbation. His nocturnal dreams furnished me an approach to his day time reveries. . . .

Indeed, negative preoccupation with erotism in the form of disgust, aversion, or desire to prosecute is a form of psychic masturbation which in our age of duplicity and false prudery is very widespread. There are persons making collection of erotic writings, pictures and nude representations of the nude, who set the police authorities on artists, volunteer to help the public prosecutor and who do these things only because they attain thereby a series of pleasurable excitations distinctly erotic. In fact, there is a form of masked onanism, which manifests itself upon the negative plane, as aversion against anything erotic. The sex purity propagandists and self-appointed sex moralists belong to this category. At best such activities are attempts at sublimating the raw erotic instincts by applying them to the service of society. I know a man who suffers from

an unconscious paraphilia, namely, he is attracted
to small children; naturally he has repressed this
tendency so that it manifests itself in the form of
a "harmless" love of children. The man is apparently preoccupied with the altruistic task of spreading sexual enlightenment among children. Of
course, it would be far fetched to call this phase of
the man's activity a form of masturbation. But
it is a fact that among the professional purists of
his type, and among the self-appointed morality
crusaders, among the demonstratively abstinent and
the vociferously ascetic, may be found the clearest
examples of masked onanism, or cryptic masturbation. Nature's laws are not to be cancelled easily
and if the realm of consciousness is being denied to
the sexual instinct, the latter finds subterfuges
whereby to slink back into the unconscious and
breaks through occasionally in spite of the subject's
struggles against the instinct. Thus, our children's
friend, mentioned above, is in the habit of patting the
children; *when doing so a warm wave surges through
his system and he grows warm,* an experience which
the man himself considers to be a manifestation of
ideal love (!)

I have been able to discover the actual substitution of masturbation in a number of compulsory
mannerisms. *Freud,* as is well known, has pointed out
that many compulsions—at one time he maintained
that all of them—stand for reproaches on account

of pleasurable sexual deeds carried out during childhood. This explanation holds true to this day of many compulsory thoughts, although it is not all-inclusive for so rich a realm as the compulsion ideas, which seems to be variously determined. Every compulsion mannerism is a compromise between instinct and repression and, as a neurotic compromise, fuses in one symptom both tendencies. Many a compulsion act is but the expression of the act of masturbation and represents a form of cryptic onanism.

Among those who suffer from compulsion neuroses, there are very frequently to be found persons who have never masturbated or who claim to have successfully "overcome" the habit. But their very compulsions prove that they are still continually preoccupied with masturbation and unable to free themselves from the habit; moreover, the clearest examples of cryptic onanism are found among these "successful" persons.

Compulsion mannerisms are particularly common among neurotics who have given up the habit on account of ethical or hygienic considerations.

The following is an illustrative case:

CASE 14. A clerk, 26 years of age, in danger of losing his position on account of his feeling of uncertainty. He must count everything over several times, and at the end he is still uncertain whether he has not made a mistake. Such manifestations of arithmomania are very common among masturbators. In their struggle against the habit they count the days that they were able to resist the temptation. Many are happy if they find that they have abstained as long as eight days and fall regularly into definite intervals. Others withstand longer, with days of prolific indulgence in masturbation between times. All such masturbators carry on regular bookkeeping account of their habit (naturally, only in their mind). Whenever they abstain from masturbating, the counting mannerism begins, though it may be subdued by masked onanism or pollutions.

Our patient did not know how much money he had received from his superior in office (a symbol of his guilt), he could not recall how many days ago a certain occurrence took place, he counted over and over the letters and packages entrusted to him, until he exhausted himself at the task, without being able to tell accurately their number in the end.

These peculiarities, combined with various hypochrondriac symptoms, became sharply aggravated during the previous two years, after he had given up masturbating. Of course, every physician called his condition neurasthenia and attributed it to the habit, a notion that corresponded with his own belief.

The patient came to me every week for a half hour to be instructed regarding his illness. He was

a very willing pupil and proved one of my outstanding successes. I cannot describe sufficiently
my amazement at the change for the better which this
patient has shown. He has got rid of all feelings of
uncertainty, he does not count any more, he is certain of himself, feels refreshed and well, has a flourishing appearance, and during the first months after
resuming masturbation gained 3 kilos in weight.
His sleep, formerly disturbed, is now deep and quiet.
The pollutions have ceased. How can the question
of the harm of masturbation be raised at all in such
a case? Why do our practitioners fail to see that
masturbation has also its uses, that masturbation is
the only possible means,—the only means available
—under existing social conditions—for the sexual
gratification of numberless widows, old maids and
confirmed bachelors?

I reproduce below, in its naïve original form, the
history of the patient mentioned above, as written by
himself two years after complete recovery and I ask
the readers to overlook the patient's excessive praises
of his psychoanalyst. This document would lose
much of its sense if it did not render truthfully
the mental attitude of the patient grateful for his
recovery.

Filled with a sense of happiness and of gratitude
I want to relate briefly my mental state before and
after my recovery.

In the first place I must state that I have achieved my cure entirely through the following means:

1. By having my repressed feelings and thoughts brought into clear consciousness so that I was freed of old inhibitions. This enabled me to attain a free viewpoint and the various unjustified qualms of conscience disappeared or ceased almost entirely.

2. By the regulation of my sexual life, specifically, through masturbation.

As the son of a minister I had to adhere strictly to the church rules and live a chaste and wholly abstinent existence. I recall that some of the more significant compulsion ideas began in my 19th year, while I was engaged in my nightly prayer. I masturbated almost daily, without attaching any particular significance to the indulgence, inasmuch as I was not properly enlightened about matters of sex because I never wanted to read about such things. Secretly, however, I reproached myself, now and then, for doing something that must be wrong; nevertheless I could not give up the habit and I repressed the evil thought. Later, when I had pollutions, I thought that I had brought upon myself some disorder through the masturbation habit and that I must be a "waster of semen," and unclean, according to the Bible. While saying my evening prayer my thoughts already turned to the habit, and I was very excited sexually, but tried to repress the feelings. That made me confused, I repeated during the prayers the same words, the same phrases, over and over. At about that same period I began to be also uncertain in my work. One day I was told all about the alleged terrible consequences of masturbation.

After that I reproached myself for having sinned and because I had damaged myself in mind and body. With all my energy I fought against the old habit, I counted the weeks, the months, and even the years during which I kept my chastity, hoping to find robust health and vitality as the reward for my abstinence. My experience was exactly the reverse. Gradually I grew more distracted and uncertain at my work, especially in accounting. I always thought I counted wrong,—that I turned over more pieces of goods than required, that I was cheating my employer. One day it occurred to me that I was a murderer. Some years ago, when my father was on his death bed, I happened to put my finger in my mouth. Now, after several years had passed, I recalled the incident, and the notion came to me that I strangled father by the act. Soon thereafter numerous other notions of murder tortured me, even though I could see before my eyes the very persons I fancied I had killed. I was unable to do a thing, because I always had a dread that I might draw upon myself consequences which would lead me to become a murderer. At times I was melancholic, sleepless, excited and very sensitive to noises. Naturally I grew more apathetic day by day, lost all self-confidence and life became but a torture to me. After four years of such self-torture, during which I was treated with bromides, cold baths, etc., and nothing helped, I decided as a last resort to take up psychotherapeutic treatment.

You have opened a new world to me. I went through analysis. Above all I saw clearly that I must regulate my sexual life, either with sexual intercourse or through masturbation. I turned temporarily to the latter means. My condition improved day by day. The treatment revealed new viewpoints to me. I learned to know my inner self and the raw instincts that thrive therein. Repressed thoughts were brought to surface. All sorts of traumatic experiences from childhood came into consciousness. I learned precisely when this or that symptom arose,—the various chaotic thoughts were traced to their roots and shown up. Thus I found out clearly what unpleasant, uncertain, melancholic and apathetic states are generated by the repression of the sexual instincts.

Of course at first the welling up of the unconscious thoughts had the effect of tremendously exciting me, but later, as I learned to perceive the deeper sense of the truths my psychoanalyst revealed I learned to view the things that lie at the bottom of the human soul with a calm eye, to understand things differently. I learned to rise above the many petty things that so often disturb human existence. I breathed more freely after every visit, during which I opened up my soul in candid confession thus easing my conscience. Every time I learned so much that was new, beautiful and charmingly true, that I felt a new zest in life. My self-confidence and my pleasure in life increased with every visit. And now I am convinced that the best means for healing the sick and for maintaining mental health is fearless confession, the candid scrutiny of one's thoughts in every direction and regular sexual life, *i.e.* the proper utilization of our surplus energies.

Looking now back over the history of my illness I perceive anew how much I have suffered. It makes me the more appreciative and grateful for the recovery of my health.

Religious scruples prevented this patient from seeking regular sexual intercourse before marriage. His attitude was highly ethical in these matters. I may add that the man—I have him under observation for eight years—has since married and is extraordinarily potent.

Such cases are far from rare. Many persons carry a latent neurosis within them which breaks out only when circumstances deprive them of their customary pleasurable objectives. When they give up masturbating their customary joy of living and zest leaves them. Ungratified persons are always unhappy. Let sexual hunger once assert itself and it sets free hidden energies,—other thwarted instincts rattle their chains. Thus one rebel in the chain-gang makes the whole gang rebellious. The psychologic investigation of criminality is of greatest significance in that connection.

This patient, too, suffered from murder impulses, in their negative form (repulsion of the thought, self-incriminating ideas), only when he turned wholly abstinent and thus became unhappy. I have had opportunity to observe that many criminals break through the ordinary inhibitions only after some tremendous deception in their love life. It is an old bit of wisdom that a happy love helps, whereas an unhappy one opens the whole Pandora box of troubles. . . .

Man wird am besten für seine Tugenden bestraft.

NIETZSCHE

IV

Case of Psychic Onanism, Descriptive Account by
Krafft-Ebing—A Case of Cryptic Onanism Cleared
up through Analysis—Fixation of a Traumatic
Scene through Onanism—Secondary Effect of Prostatic Massage—Therapeutic Efficacy of Magnetism
depends on Sexuality—A Woman treated by a Mag-
netizer—Influence of Massage on Eros—The En-
terocleaner—Gonorrhœa and Neurosis—Case of a
Miraculous Cure through Prostatic Massage—
Analysis of the Masturbator's "Guilty" Conscience
—Masturbation as Symbol for Every Form of Guilt
—Illustration of the Shifting of Responsibility—
The Contrary Influence of Taboos and Proscrip-
tions—Danger and Guilt as Provocatives of Grati-
fication—Prophylaxis of Early Masturbation—
Educational Blunders—Onanism and Potentia—
Onanism an Infantile Regression.

IV

One is most punished for one's virtues.

NIETZSCHE

When the harmless character of masturbation is explained the patients may be seen incredulously shaking their heads and often they refuse to believe the truth. They cannot give up the idea of playing with danger; or else, they fear masturbation because the practice is associated in their case with the oft-mentioned phantasies. In fact, the habit permits a shifting which often masks the most interesting conflicts. Moreover, mechanically induced masturbation is not alone the possible source of a troubled conscience. That psychic onanism, too, may cause such manifestations is shown by the next case.

The struggle against psychic masturbation is even more relentless than against the physical act, because in that connection the forbidden images which continually press forth are not so easily held back through the various ordinary inhibitions.

The next case also discloses plainly pollutions as a substitute for masturbation, *i.e.* the displacement of conscious masturbation by unconscious onanism.

153

Krafft-Ebing [1] relates the following characteristic case:

CASE 15.   Miss X., 30 years old, with hereditary taint in the family, neuropathic since childhood, assures us that she has had lascivious images as early as during her 6th year, and that she has always been in the habit of indulging in them.   In time this developed into actual psychic onanism and in later years her condition was aggravated by *neurasthenia sexualis*.   Patient suspected a relationship between her trouble and the bad habit.   *Bock's* popular book supplied her the desired explanation as well as tremendous excitation.   Family misfortunes increased her troubles.   Then the patient gave up her bad habit but thereafter her condition at once grew visibly worse.   She became nervous, very excitable, and dysthymic; her sleep was troubled with ugly, lascivious dreams which left her ungratified; spinal irritation, anemia, dysmenorrhœa.   The lure of the male sex and of marriage, always weak in her case, sunk to a minimum; on the other hand the patient became more and more strongly the victim of a genital orgasm, in itself far from pleasurable, and even somewhat painful,—a condition not unlike priapism in the male.   Nightly pollutions, in the sense that the patient woke up in the midst of her lascivious dreams with a certain pleasurable feeling and a humidity of the external genitalia.   After such

[1] *Psychopathia Sexualis*, 14th edition.   Stuttgart, Enke, 1912.

pollutions for days she felt exhausted, depressed, and there was a painful spinal irritation. Eventually the nocturnal pollutions took place without the accompaniment of sensuous dreams and finally she began to have similar experiences during the day. In the midst of signs of considerable resistance the patient finally discloses these facts to her physician. She is anemic, emaciated, restless, and depressed. She sleeps but little, her sleep is not refreshing, feels exhausted and miserable, and complains of paralgic pains in the region of the lumbo-sacral plexus. The deep reflexes are increased. She fears spinal trouble and explains her dread as due to her psychic onanism, a practice in which she has indulged for years. Has never masturbated. Her chief complaint is an almost continual unrest, and the excitation in the genital region. The latter feeling was not unlike the craving in the gastric region when one is hungry. Around her genitalia (objective examination, negative) she feels a torturing burning, heat, unrest, and pulsations,—as if some clock mechanism had been set loose there. Pleasurable thought in that connection only very rarely. This sexual neurosis has a tremendous depressing influence on her. She finds transitory peace only when the condition leads to pollution, but subsequently that in turn only aggravates her neuropathic troubles. Her sufferings are at their worst during her menstrual period. Bathing in 23°-19°

R, suppositories of Camphor monobrom. 0.6, with Extr. belladonn. 0.04, Sod. brom. 3.0 to 4.0 evenings, powder of Camphora 0.1, Lupulin 0.5, Extr. secal. 0.08, twice daily, greatly improved the patient and gave her complete rest for days. In that way she regained her shattered confidence in the future as well as a certain measure of mental balance.

In this case we also note a marked aggravation of the symptoms as soon as the patient resumed her fight against psychic onanism,—an indulgence which yielded her but partial gratification. Her pollutions finally helped her. She substituted unconscious psychic onanism for the conscious habit.

How unsatisfactory these histories recorded in purely descriptive form! The various forms of "unconscious onanism" may be revealed only after thorough investigation in the analytic sense. But such an investigation is not easy. *The task requires a knowledge of technique as well as experience. Hence the unbridgeable cleft between the conscientious analyst and the physician who, without a knowledge of the technique, attempts to test the principles that govern psychoanalysis and its results.*

It is interesting that pain may also mask a cryptic masturbation. The recognition of orgasms is a task not easily learned, and even the analyst meets cases which leave him in doubt. And I repeat: only the phantasies accompanying the masturbation act fully reveal its true significance.

The following case is in many respects very interesting:

CASE 16. A 42-year-old woman is referred to me by a country practitioner on account of abdominal pains. The woman suffers from these pains for the past nine years. It is a strange neuralgia in the appendiceal region, radiating towards the bladder and back. MacBurney's point is not sensitive to pressure. But there is sensitiveness, growing worse, as one approaches the median line. The patient has been treated by various methods. In Vienna the pain was ascribed to a retroflexion of the uterus. Finally a famous gynecologist advised her to have hysterectomy. She readily agreed in order to get rid of the pains. At first the results seemed splendid. But three weeks after the operation the pains began anew and with greater ferocity. Then the specialists concluded that the pains were of a nervous origin and they began medicating her with bromides, valerian, electricity, etc. Nothing did any good. Dr. H., a general practitioner, having read my book, *Nervous Anxiety States*, referred the patient to me with the remark that the case was undoubtedly psychogenetic, adding that he was unable to find the cause.

Analysis of the case revealed a significant fact
during the very first consultation hour. One-half
year before the attacks of abdominal pains began,
she had a sensuous dream (which recurred later),
and on that occasion she experienced orgasm for the
first time in her life. During her marital relations
she had always been anesthetic. Though she had
married at 23 years of age, she began to "feel,"
only at the age of 33, roused by a dream. Very
much worried and excited over the experience—in
spite of its pleasurable quality—she inquired among
her intimate women friends what it meant and she
felt reassured when she was told that it was a normal
occurrence, that every woman must have the experience. And that at 33 years of age! But now she
asserts that there exists a certain relationship between the pleasure and the pains. *She has found
that the pains are always worse after she has had a
"sweet" dream.* (It seemed that the pains were a
punishment for indulging in some forbidden pleasure!)

The pleasurable dream in question she could not
recall. She thinks she may have dreamed of having
sexual intercourse with her husband; sometimes, that
she was lying on his breast and suckling. *At other
times something else which she could not remember.*
Even now she experiences no pleasure during sexual
embrace with her husband.

Finally she discloses another remarkable confession: *when the pains are very tremendous she must have recourse to massage. That relieves the pains, and if she also experiences a mild pleasurable sensation at the time, she is certain to have a "sweet" dream that night.*

At the next sitting she tells me about her disappointment in the results of the operation. She had been told that with the internal sexual organs removed she will no longer be a woman. That is why she joyfully consented to have the operation. She struggled against sexuality aiming at purity. For three weeks she was happy having no "sweet" dream. Then she had three pollution dreams in one night. The very next day the abdominal pain returned, with greater intensity than ever, and with it also a deep depression.

We note that the case turns out to be an interesting instance of cryptic onanism. The self-reproach linked with the pains or, rather, with the accompanying orgasm, is extraordinarily strong, apparently depending on some accompanying phantasy. But how get at the phantasy in question? The patient was to stay in Vienna but a week.

I attempted hypnosis. It was but a partial success. The patient excused her inhibition, remarking that she was afraid she might say something during the hypnosis that would compromise her. Asked what that remark might refer to, she gave evasive answer: there was nothing for her to hide! Though she has been married 23 years she is as innocent as newly fallen snow! Her husband himself was surprised at her lack of experience and her ignorance of sexual matters.

Following day she disclosed unexpectedly something of which she had not thought for years. She had forgotten altogether the incident in question. The memory thereof suddenly struck her mind at the end of a dream which is as follows:

I go to a candy store to buy some candy. Instead of candy the saleswoman gives me ink. I bespot myself all over. Then I take a few baths to wash myself clean.

The patient has no associations to this dream and I call her attention to the fact that she must have experienced something in her life that made her think she had bespotted herself. She is now trying to wash herself clean. . . . That was the meaning of the dream.

She gives the stereotypic answer: no experience whatever, she knows nothing of the kind. Then I ask her if anything has ever happened to her in a candy store. As to that she answers: "In a candy store, no; but suddenly there comes to me something I had forgotten altogether. I was seven years of age; an apprentice boy who was working for my father enticed me with candy to a dark corner.

There he told me he would show me something sweet. He lifted my dress and did something to me."

"Did you tell your parents?"

"No, because I was very much ashamed. But I begged father to dismiss the apprentice, I could not bear to see him. I avoided him and always kept him at a distance whenever we happened to be again alone. But I was seventeen years of age when he left."

"Did you see him again after that?"

"Yes, but I had been married a long time at the time."

"How old were you?"

"It was the year of my miscarriage, therefore I was 33."

"The same year in which your pains and pollutions began?"

"Yes,—same year. I went from home on a journey to Vienna that time."

At this juncture I must intercalate an observation. We call such an occurrence, a trauma. The significance of such traumata has been decidedly overstressed by the earlier writings of the Freudian school. Nevertheless we must guard against underestimating the lasting effect of so tremendous an experience. Several consequences are possible. The trauma may be borne well and the individual overcomes the shock. Or the subject becomes later neurotic and subsequently utilizes the trauma in the

dynamics of his neurosis. The experience may prove
an inciter to the flighty minded as readily as it may
become the cause of morbid hyper-morality. It may
act as an inducement for its repetition or as a warning against its repetition. In the latter case the
children are driven to excessive modesty and on
account of the violence of the occurrence, the brutal-
ity of the experience, they become a prey to the
antisexual instinct. The craving for its repetition
is cancelled by the counter-endeavor to avoid the
experience. A trauma of this kind has driven more
than one girl into the cloister. I know a number of
such cases. Or else, it may lead to the overemphasis
of chastity to an unnatural extent. That was the
case in the present instance. The little girl became
excessively bashful, timid and chaste. In her heart
she entertained the hope that the apprentice would
make up for his sin by an offer of marriage. For
she loved the apprentice boy and could never forget
him! She considered herself a wife and married at
23 years only after considerable hesitation. But the
boy remained single. She could still indulge in the
phantasy of a sin-cleansing marriage. In her old
home town she saw for the first time the boy as a
married man, having heard that he had married.
She returned to her own home and a prolific vaginal
discharge compelled her to go to Vienna. That
vaginal discharge was already a symptom of her

excessive excitability. The accumulated, long damned up libido sought an outbreak.

Only at the following sitting did I find out that she was "massaged" while in Vienna. The patient localized her pains deeply in front and in the back. At once I thought of bi-manual examination, but this she denied. During the physical examinations by the doctors she has never felt either pain or pleasure.

On the following day, however, she recalled a bi-manual examination. She had hardly been aware of what was going on while the hands of the great, big, strong doctor manipulated inside her. Her uterus was found bent backwards and she was advised to take massage treatments. There were blue dermal discolorations on her and that night she could not sleep on account of her excitement. Before the massage treatments she always trembled, as if facing some terrible ordeal.

Briefly I find out that the massage treatments had a tremendously exciting effect upon her and that after a considerable time they roused in her feelings distinctly sensuous, but also associated with pain.

Now the case becomes clear. During that first coitus the girl child experienced a strong sensation of pleasure along with the pain. The disparity between the big phallus and the infantile vagina was too great. After marriage she was disappointed during the very first bridal night by the relatively small *membrum virile*. It left her anesthetic. The memory of the big phallus seen in her childhood disturbed the current impression. The approach of the marital partner recalled anew the buried memory of the old experience. The massage treatments reproduced the old traumatic incident in a masked form. A big thing (the masseur's great hand) handling her parts, clearly a reminder of the wholly forgotten infantile onanism. Her dammed up sexuality broke through again. Frequently she had dreams which repeated these massage treatments.

Now we understand *why the pains cease when she massages herself, and why she is certain to induce a pollution in that manner.* Her self-massage reminded her of the professional massage treatments and of the infantile childhood trauma, and in her sleep her hand carried out the onanistic act.

The unconscious onanism need not trouble her conscience, inasmuch as she cannot help it. Nevertheless her mind is very uneasy over it; this is because through her first lover and her physician she is untrue to her husband.

These fancies are also mixed with death thoughts, whereby all the obstacles between herself and her first lover are cleared out of the way.

That is the explanation of her pains. We see that the country doctor was right when he assumed that the trouble had psychogenetic roots. And we shudder to think how many gynecologic operations are thus needlessly performed.

Here again our inquiry leads us to a pathogenetic occurrence which became fixed through onanism.[2] It seems that all the capacity for libido was concentrated on this scene. We shall discuss a number of such cases in our study of the *Sexual Frigidity of Woman*. The effect of the analysis upon these frigid, fascinated women is to make them aware of the traumatic occurrence so that their fixed libido becomes released and available for other forms of sexual expression. I should not be surprised if this patient should now experience orgasm during intercourse with her husband. I have not heard further from her.

The clinical history of this case teaches us something about the erotic effect of medical treatments.

Every experienced physician knows that certain therapeutic procedures produce an erotic reaction on patients. The very manner in which women behave during a careful examination betrays at once what they think of their physician. In fact to many of the patients he is always but a man. They exhibit all sorts of inhibitions, partly deliberate and partly with secret intent; they emphasize their bashfulness, insist that the physician should turn around, or look away, or that he should examine only a

[2] Masturbation is the fixative which sets permanently the lightly thrown up pastel pictures, or which at least protects them against the ravages of time.

certain region of the body, and ask whether they
"must" take off their shirt. The greater the ease
with which a woman undresses herself the less she
thinks of the physical examination as an erotic act.
That many women have themselves examined entirely
for erotic reasons, is a fact I can corroborate
through my professional experience dating back to
the time when I was engaged in general practice.
Indeed, an elderly, very reserved, lady once said to
me: "If you will allow me a bit of advice for the
good of your practice, let me tell you: always give
as thorough a physical examination as possible to
the women who come to you and while at it preserve
your professional attitude. The women expect it;
they feel slighted if it is not done. I have always
heard women criticize the physicians who either because of lack of time or on account of bashfulness
examined them but superficially. I believe the women
derive a secret pleasure from such things though
they won't admit it."

That lady was right. All such excitations belong
to the category of *Lust ohne Schuld,—pleasure without guilt*. But I do not propose to go into these
daily occurrences at length. Of greater importance,
by far, seems to me the fact that the gynecologist—
without knowing it—uses erotic means in his therapeutic armamentarium. Even ordinary physical examination is for many women a sort of trauma with
which their mind is constantly preoccupied there-

after; bi-manual manipulation, or massage, very often is but a form of allerotic activity, which we have already identified as masturbation. Experienced gynecologists are aware of that and they take all sorts of precautionary measures. But the women, after getting accustomed to massage, are sometimes very unhappy if they must give up the treatment. In my own practice I recall a woman whom I massaged very carefully for an exudate. When I saw plainly that the treatment had an exciting effect upon her so that it actually induced orgasm, I advised the patient to give up the treatment. But she insisted stubbornly that it was the only thing which helped her condition and . . . sought the services of another physician. Some women hide their orgasm under all sorts of expressions of pain, the "pain" causes them to turn red in the face,—they insist that the procedure is extremely painful and unpleasant to them. During the orgasm, to cover the character of their experience, they wince "with pain."

These various forms of sexual expression are highly prized by some patients. For instance, I was told by a specialist of women that among his patients there were a number of old maids who came regularly every month, once or twice, for physical examination. The examinations seemed to furnish a point of vantage for their phantasy indulgences. Undoubtedly the examination stands for the well

known "bit of reality" which the neurotic needs as a
"banner" for his fancies. That is why many patients conjure up the familiar notion that the physician has carried out or has attempted sexual assault
on them, an accusation that but very seldom proves
true. The women in question visit the physician
with the expectation,—they anticipate an assault.
Often the phantastic accusation is but a punishment
for the physician's proper behavior, an attitude
which some women resent as insulting. Every woman
prizes the fact that she is desired. She always
acknowledges with gratitude the recognition of her
charms provided this is not done in too raw a form.
Many respectable women leave the physician's office
in anger if he has failed to regard them as women,
i.e. if he has behaved indifferently towards their
charms.

During the analysis these manifestations become
very plain. The patients seek the physician's love
and they dream repeatedly of situations involving
physical examination by their physician. The patients display considerable adroitness in the attempt
of inducing their consultant to break the first rule
of analytic practice which reads: patients who are
psychoanalyzed must not be given physical examinations during the treatment. But they do very
much want to be examined by the analyst! They
point to something trivial under their elbow, or on
their breast, and ask to be examined because they do

not care to go to another physician "for so small a thing." They insist that their gastric trouble is undoubtedly organic. Let the analyst examine them once and he will be convinced. They positively have a growth, a ball is forming inside, and other such nonsense is insisted upon, to beguile the analyst out of his attitude of reserve. Indeed, I have had repeatedly the following experience: after getting through with the analytic treatment, the women would say: "Now that we are through with the analysis you can treat me internally." During the beginnings of my psychoanalytic practice a woman came to me at the end of the psychotherapeutic treatment persistently begging me to give her a gynecologic examination. She had confidence in me alone and would not allow another doctor so much as to touch her. She was afraid she had cancer. I was still in general practice at the time and did not know all the ways and subterfuges of patients. I examined her, found no indications of cancer, and after that never saw her again. Obviously what she had hoped was that the sight of her hidden charms would so overwhelm me as to make me her obedient slave. She would have probably repulsed me, had I made any advances, because what she wanted was to leave me in the lurch while preserving on her part the attitude of a conqueror. Vanquished, instead, according to her scale of measurements, she left my office, never to show her face to me again.

Another case had a similar outcome. A woman
wanted to appoint me her family physician and first
pressed me for a gynecologic examination. I had
not the slightest suspicion what she expected of me.
But she never came back. Subsequently she told a
woman friend that I was "no man."

That the discussion of erotic themes acts as a
sexual stimulant is a fact which every analyst must
bear in mind. I know that there are physicians who
not only talk of sexual matters quite openly with
their patients but they do so using the common
expressions. . . . I consider it a great advantage
that I can speak of such matters without hurting
the patient's sensibilities.

A great deal depends on the art and manner in
which one talks to the patient. I avoid, in particular, all unpleasant questioning, such as *Hoche* and
Näcke imagine necessary in psychoanalysis. I suggest nothing to the patient, allowing him to talk
freely. I aid the recall of memories and treat the
statements so that the patient, man or woman, need
not feel uncomfortable. And I must not overlook to
mention that many patients have the notion that it
is necessary only to speak out every hidden sexual
thought, that anything else does not matter. Thereupon they produce a mass of erotic phantasies,
which keep repeating themselves, so that it seems
that all that is necessary is to analyze these phantasies. Sometimes this wholesale production of

erotic fancies is but a form or resistance, an attempt
to reduce the analysis *ad absurdum*. For example,
an extraordinarily delicate-minded woman came to
me to be treated for compulsion neurosis. She began
at once by telling me that she could not disclose her
thoughts. Her thoughts had to do with my sexuality. It was a way of dodging the psychoanalysis.
She had heard a woman friend say: "You will have
to hear and say awful things. Think of it, you will
have to speak out every bit of your thoughts. . . ."
I listened for a few days to her fancy weaving, then
I said: "From now on you are absolved from the
rule of telling everything that comes to your mind.
I mean, you need not express any further the
thoughts that pertain to me. It is not at all necessary for me to hear everything. You may say, or
speak out, anything you please." From that day all
phantasies referring to me left her completely. She
had met the requirement of the analysis with a compulsion of her own whereby the analysis was to be
reduced *ad absurdum*. But after that we made good
progress with the analysis and it resulted in a great
therapeutic success. Everything assumed in time its
proportionate importance so that it was possible to
give to sexual matters also their due share of attention and no more.

I now return to my general theme. Many wonderful cures ascribed to some particular therapeutic
means are due to erotic excitations. I have seen so-

called neurasthenia give way to long continued massaging of the prostate.

Experienced urologists sometimes find that they cannot get rid of patients who are treated by prostatic massage. These patients come back again and again and are only too willing to submit to the ordeal. They insist all the time that the procedure is painful and unpleasant to them, but that they gladly submit to the massage treatments, if they can only be cured. . . . And they keep coming back for the indispensable massage treatments. . . . The treatment of gonorrhœa by means of bogies may also bring about erotic excitation in certain patients suffering from urethral erotism (*Sadger*), and in whom, consequently, the urethra is an erogenous zone. This explains the fixation of many gonorrhœic patients on their gonorrhœa and on their physician. Masturbation through the introduction of various objects into the urethra is by no means uncommon. Every experienced urologist meets such cases and often they require serious operations.

Various other procedures, massages, rubbings, passive exercises, baths, etc., have a similar effect. I need hardly emphasize that sun-bathing sanitaria (Solaria) are a gathering place for exhibitionists and for others who are either consciously or unconsciously homosexual. Less well known in this respect is the effect of hydrotherapeutic procedures, which in some cases owe their refreshing effect to their erotic value. It is not necessary to refer specifically to particular procedures, such as the famous Kühne baths, a procedure which obviously brings about erotic stimulation and stands for an onanistic act under the guise of treatment. On their part the patients are happy thus to have recourse to a legitimate means for deceiving the world (as well as themselves). What they are after is something whereby to allay their conscience and at the same time to keep on indulging, on the *Lust ohne Schuld*— pleasure-without-guilt—principle.

As an illustration of unconscious erotic excitation we quote a description of the magnetic healing procedure, as reported by *Meissner* in the *Therapeutische Monatshefte:*

"According to the patient's own testimony," states the author, "when the electrodes touch his body, the sensitive patient about to be magnetised presently perceives a strange something in his body, emanating not from the magnetic apparatus, but from the vital magnetism of the manipulating hand. But that something strange is not to be thought as making itself felt in the patient's body as definitely as the electricity that may be carried over artificially by means of certain apparatus. It makes its presence felt, rather, as something more delicate, something much more subdued, as a soft wafting of air,

as a mild wind, slowly caressing the respective body
parts, or as a subdued creepiness, a mild drowsiness,
as soft as the onrush of blood under the nails,
spreading like a soft, warm, mild, or cool stream
through the individual parts, or through the whole
body, depending on the direction of the magnetic
streams as governed by the manner of the laying on
of the hands. The sensations are nearly always not
unlike those engendered by a penetrating but mild
electric wave and associated with a most comforting
sense of general well being. Sometimes I have had
in the winter season patients half undressed coming
into a room where the temperature was no more
than 13°-R., and although at first they were shaking
with the cold, after I began my magnetic passing of
hands, I heard those properly sensitized declare
with astonishment that they felt their body becoming surcharged with a warmth not unlike that of the
Summer season; other patients suffering from unpleasant body heat during magnetisation perceive a
refreshing sensation of coolness."

Of course, such miracles of magnetism are the
miracles of love and erotism. Everything is possible
through sexuality. These apparently supernatural
effects are produced through erotic excitation. Who
doubts the stimulating effect of sexuality in any
form? On the other hand such excitations may also
prove harmful if they awaken unfulfillable wishes or
if they fail to lead to a releasing orgasm.

An extremely interesting case from my personal observation illustrates these relations in a particularly clear manner:

CASE 17. Mrs. R. S., 37 years of age, consults me for sleeplessness. She wants to be hypnotized. She has not slept for weeks. She must have sleep. But as soon as she goes to bed, thoughts begin to torture her: "You won't sleep and you will look badly in the morning!" As soon as that comes to her mind, she becomes restless. Her nervousness grows and she is finally compelled to seek sleep by means of drugs,— Adalin, 1.0 g., or Veronal, 0.5. "My sleeplessness," she tells me, "began when I first started to be treated by a magnetizer. Two years ago I suffered from nervous gastric trouble and, at the suggestion of a friend, I sought the services of Dr. B., a magnetizer. I believe in magnetism. Through Dr. B.'s magnetic treatments I experienced a warm wave passing from the stomach out over my whole body. Three weeks ago I again sought Dr. B. because I suffered from nervous shivering all over my body and palpitation. I found out that the poor man had died. So I went to another magnetizer, Dr. X., who promised to cure me in a few days. I was terribly restless by the time I looked him up. My whole body was shaking. He had me sit in a chair and he passed his hand over my whole body. He was magnetically more powerful than Dr. B. I felt at once a hot wave, melting through my whole body. I felt hot and cold in waves. Dr. X. said: 'You are remarkably sensitive to magnetism. You are an excellent medium.' The very next day he asked me to accompany him to his house. I was under his magnetic influence. I pranced all over the room, at Dr. X.'s bidding. But I did not sleep through the whole night. Dr. X. said: 'That is the crisis. You will soon be well.' But my excitation grew all the time and once I was so restless in the presence of Dr. X. that he could not continue the magnetic treatment. He said: 'You are too restless today for the magnetic treatment. Let us go to a moving picture show.' We went there. I sat next to him and felt his magnetic influence so strongly that I could not take in the show at all."

The patient's previous history is as follows: Mrs. R. S. was precocious in sexual matters already as a small child. She masturbated since her childhood days and has masturbated in the company of girl friends. At 13 years of age she was intimate with a girl friend who performed cunnilingus on her. She was very coquettish and had no thought of anything but men, paraphilias. . . . She was greedily reading pornographic literature. At 17 she became acquainted with a man with whom she had intercourse and who subsequently wanted to marry her. She seldom experienced orgasm with him but that did not trouble her in the least because she always achieved orgasm *post coitum*, by means of masturbation. At

19 she became acquainted with another man to whom
she felt spiritually much more strongly attracted.
He proposed marriage. But he was an army officer
and as she did not have the required dower, marriage
was not possible. They lived happily in free union.
She loved him because he was a lovely, fine man and
very good to her in every way. She knew that he
was true to her and that he would marry her as soon
as circumstances permitted. Next her disposition
underwent a radical change. She became serious-
minded, turning her attention to art and literature.
She was also glad that of late she was experiencing
orgasm during coitus more often than formerly.

As a consequence she made up her mind to abandon the masturbation habit. She actually kept this
resolution. For two years she did not masturbate.
After turning abstinent her nervous gastric trouble
set in, soon leaving her and in its place she began to
suffer from general nervousness.

Her trouble has something to do with the war
situation. Her lover was at the front. She was all
the time alone with her sister living abstinently.
Her temptation to masturbate was very strong. Yet
she withstood very bravely that temptation.

But now the theories of Dr. X., the magnetizer,
troubled her. After one week Dr. X. told her: "You
need a man; your trouble is due to your abstinence!"
That excited her tremendously. "I did not want to
masturbate again," she tells me. "For nothing in

the world! I was happy to be rid of the habit. The magnetizer's words roused me terribly. His hand manipulations quieted me but for a moment, then I felt worse. I ran around on the streets and was almost ready to give myself to any strange man. I was mad with excitation and cravings. Now my nerves are all to pieces, my sleep is gone. . . . Help me. . . . I must not be untrue to my man! Rather would I take my life! If you would only read the letters he sends me from the front. He wants to marry me as soon as he comes back. How could I take a lover and deceive him!"

Certainly no advice could be worse, and no physician has a right to give such advice. Were the woman not struggling against her sexuality, were she not so "moral" and neurotic, she would discover the corresponding advice for herself. Such advice can only increase the inner conflict and make wholly a wreck out of the nervous woman. She is religious, goes to church daily, and to confession. She regards her relations with the man as a marriage, and it is that, in the best sense of the word. . . .

She tells about her sleepless nights. She says that she wakes up her sister who sits by her bedside and must caress her. We find out that she is a particularly good subject for magnetism because the skin is her erogenous zone. Her lover brings on orgasm in her only after first caressing her for a long time. . . . It is a typical infantile disposition.

After a few more hours of consultations I can form in my mind a clear picture of her neurosis. Many determinants were involved in complex trouble. She still hears from her first lover. When he left he told her that he would always wait for her and never marry. She preferred the second lover because the latter was in a better financial position and of a milder temperament. The first one was quick tempered, he gambled, drank and was unreliable at times. . . . The other one was mild and soft. The one was a man of intellect, the other a man of feelings. It is often noticeable that raw men draw the women more closely to themselves, they exert a greater charm on women than those of soft temperament. They more concretely than others suggest the thought of being "manly." The second lover, though an army officer, had something effeminate about him. And that is a feature that played a great rôle in her neurosis. Her psychic conflict revolved over an instantaneous thought, which, of course, she promptly repressed,—a thought which may be expressed as follows: *Should your lover fall at the front, you would be free to marry the first one who is still waiting for you! But are you still young and attractive enough to appeal to him?* Her looking glass daily testified to her: *You are!* She was afraid of growing old, afraid of face wrinkles, afraid of marks of ugliness! She had not been too insistent about marriage precisely because she was still hope-

fully holding on to the other lover. Marriage would
have put an end to this fiction, or phantasy. She
needed that scrap of reality in order to hitch her
phantasies on to it. She did not want to think of
these things,—of the death wish! Hence the
thought: You must sleep and forget these things!
You should sleep through the war period. Her
cravings increased because all her instincts were
chained down through her abstinence. Then, along
came the doctor with the suggestion that she needs a
man. Her lover was at the front,—it meant finding
another man. At once the thought came to her:
who should that other man be but the first lover,
whom she had never forgotten,—since no woman
forgets the man who was the first to enjoy her
virginity, the first to introduce her to the mysteries
of love?

Thus there arose the compulsion idea: *you cannot
sleep! and tomorrow you will look ugly! You will
look old!* She had to keep herself young for the
sake of the other man. This compulsive thought
held her in its clutches,—through the whole day she
had no other idea in her mind than sleep. . . . Sleep
meant, forgetting the whole conflict.

Another determinant of her condition was traceable to her infancy and her homosexual trend. The
cunnilingus that her friend carried out on her was
an unforgettable incident. Living together with her
sister must have roused the wish to be similarly

gratified by the sister. She said spontaneously to me: "I do not think it is well for me to live with my sister. We fight all day long and at night I call her to my bedside to have her pat me and caress me like a child. But I cannot live alone. I always have to have some one near me. Where could I find a person for that?" . . .

I know nothing about the patient's subsequent history. But I think we may assume that she went back to her magnetizer, for she assured me during the last visit that, after all, the magnetizer helped her. Had the doctor not referred to her wanting a man she might have regained her health. I suspected at once that her emotional attachment to Dr. X. will drive her back to him. She told me wonderful things about his strength and prowess. But that she wishes her lover to die so as to get the other man is something she did not want to acknowledge. She shakes when she receives a letter. She trembles with dread when she scans over the casualty lists. One might think that she does this out of anxiety over her lover,—because of her great love for him. But it is merely the staging of a self-deceiving comedy. She needs an energetic man, fearing she might yield to the love for woman. . . .

Listening to her account of the effect of the magnetizer's treatment we recognize at once that his hand stroking undoubtedly roused this highly sensitive woman who is in a state of libidinous expectancy

and whose skin is markedly erogenous. The enforced abstinence and the abandonment of masturbation have deprived her of the customary outlets
for her sensuous cravings. She succeeded in transferring her libido almost entirely upon the heterosexual path. The enforced abstinence raised new
problems for her. Masturbation and sexual intercourse were out of the question. The magnetizer's
stroking hand roused so many fervid cravings that
she could not sleep. Then the magnetizer's explanations, and his hints at the possibility of cure through
intercourse with other men, almost threw the highly
erotic woman off her balance. The fore-pleasure of
the hot wave generated by the magnetizer's erotic
excitation proved no longer sufficient for her. She
craved stronger gratification. This woman was a
fanatic believer in massage. She has had all sorts of
pains massaged away. Female operators had a particularly strong exciting effect upon her,—she grew
almost feverish under their manipulations.

Many massage cures may work their miracles in
the same way.

I want to call attention also to the erotizing hand
strokings as a procedure in inducing hypnosis and
to the sexual influence of waking suggestion which,
in the case of masochistically disposed persons, may
even lead to orgasm. Hypnosis involves subjection
to the partner by way of fascination (*Ferenczi*) and
is sometimes taken advantage of by unscrupulous

hypnotizers. Of course, the accusations of hysterical women who claim to have been seduced during hypnosis must be scrutinized very critically. These women often mistake expectations and phantasies for alleged realities, thus revenging themselves on the hypnotizer who fails to fulfill their expectations. But, that hypnotic, and even spiritistic, seances may act as an erotic stimulus cannot be denied.

A new apparatus, said to be very popular, the so-called entero-cleaner, is capable of rousing great erotic excitation. It involves the use of large quantities of tepid water for an "internal bath," *i.e.* rectal enema. It is said to be very useful in constipation and other bowel troubles. But with its therapeutic uses are linked also certain erotic excitations, as may be learned from a study of the subject in *Dr. Anton Brosch's* monograph, *Das Subæquale Bad* (Franz Deuticke, Leipzig und Wien, 1912).

Brosch describes the effect of his entero-cleaner as follows:

"The hydropathic stream rouses in the mucous membrane of anus and rectum a pleasant, light prickling, massage-like sensation, not unlike the hydropathic stream thrown against the external skin. Apparently the rectal and anal mucous membranes are provided with particularly sensitive nerve ends which enhance this highly pleasurable feeling-sensation in the parts. It should be noted that this sensation is wholly different from the excitation having a sexual character. The use of cool and even of cold water for the internal bath, on the contrary, has a remarkably quieting effect upon the sexual organs.

"The cool internal bath to a certain extent reproduces artificially the mechanism of the orgasm; it brings about all the physical and psychical advantages of the orgasm without the disadvantages of sexual intercourse.

"This artificial orgasm *sine usum genitalium* furnishes us the key for unlocking the reason why the internal bath has such a refreshing effect upon mind and body.

"Should any doubters still demand proof that this artificial orgasm is almost identical with the natural orgasm they may find such proof in the two features that are shared alike by the artificial and the natural orgasm, namely, the accompanying gratifying sense of well-being, and the complete subsiding of the libido after the procedure."

It is gratifying to note that the author has had the courage openly to preconize the curative effect of sexuality. Such candor is a sign of progress. And I can easily imagine the physician prescribing such internal baths, with the deliberate intention of helping some poor tortured fellow to attain orgasm, and that without hiding the reason. Think of the great army of bowel hypochondriacs, for whom the anus is literally the "axis of the world" in which they are most interested! But the patients do not want to have the promise of gratification openly held out to them. They want to attain the gratification secretly,—without the coöperation of their conscious will.

At the same time I must point out that such stimulation is not without its dangers. Many persons must feel worse after these procedures; these are "over moral" persons, who rebel even at the prospect of such "subcutaneous" pleasurable sensations. For so drastic a therapeutic procedure the usual rule holds true: it does work alike in all cases.

For one thing, there is the great danger of habit formation. As is well known, the more serious neuroses break forth when we are deprived of some customary gratification. *Brosch* now sees the miracles of sexual gratification. Before long he may be confronted with the horrors of abstinence. Such procedures, in fact, do not effect a permanent result. Temporarily the results may be very splendid. That much may be admitted. But what becomes of the poor patients after the orgasms cease? Every form of gratification requires repetition as well as enhancement. The patients accustom themselves to the entero-cleaner, they become slaves to it.

A great deal more remains to be said on this theme,—erotic stimulation as a therapeutic factor. How many cures in sanitaria and in private practice are the result of emotional transference? Our

chapter would grow endlessly if we attempted to
cover every phase of the subject. I must limit myself to the few examples already discussed. I think it
is more proper as well as more dignified for physicians to appreciate that sexual stimuli have their
therapeutic value than that they should deceive their
patients and themselves about it.

This matter interests me also for another reason.
I hold persistently the view that masturbation is
harmless. These mechanistic procedures usually
prove onanistic or masturbatory in character. Here
we find certain procedures having a highly important
therapeutic value. For centuries masturbation has
been invested with unspeakable odium in the popular
mind. Therapeutic use does away with this odium.
It raises the erotic stimulation to the rank of a
healing factor, saving the subject from all self-
reproach as well as from all sense of guilt. If the
entero-cleaner has such wonderful effects, there is no
reason why any onanistic procedure may not bring
about similar results. There are other ways for the
patient to stimulate his anal mucosa. . . .

Indeed, such instances are far from rare. I refer
here briefly to a few cases taken from among the
many that I could quote from my own practice,
because these cases illustrate the operation of unconscious masturbation and because, incidentally,
they throw light on the question: "How are therapeutic results achieved?"

I knew a specialist who showed that neurasthenia
frequently developed in the course of chronic gonorrhœa. Among the neurastheniacs there are always
a large number of sufferers who have either gone
through, or are being treated for, a severe gonorrhœa. Particularly chronic prostatitis is either
mentioned in the anamnesis or often found when the
neurotics are examined, therefore it is not surprising
that many specialists are led to assume a direct
relationship between the two conditions and to preconize the toxic theory of neurasthenia.[3a]

The same colleague has told me of wonderful
cures of neurasthenia by means of prolonged massage treatments. I have already mentioned that
persons with suppressed homosexuality seem unable
to get rid of their venereal infection and keep going
to specialists for treatment. Not infrequently the
gonorrhœal infection induces disgust of woman and
the latent homosexuality thus becomes manifest.

I myself was predisposed to consider the specialist's views correct, inasmuch as I suspected that
erotic factors influenced the cure in such cases and
would have gladly availed myself of an opportunity
to test the results. Just then chance brought me in
touch with one of his ex-patients, a man who had me
called to his house on account of a pronounced
agoraphobia.

[3a] On the relationship between prostatitis and neurasthenia,
cp. my *Nervous Anxiety States,* trsl. *Van Teslaar.*

CASE 18. Mr. Adam suffers from fear of open spaces (agoraphobia) for the past few years so that he is unable to leave his room. He gives a lengthy history of illness, in the course of which he particularly emphasizes, among other troubles, anal cramps and similar symptoms, constipation, anal fissures, neurasthenia and gonorrhœa. He had me called because he heard of me as a famous hypnotizer and thought I could relieve him of his agoraphobia through "suggestion." He has already consulted a number of famous hypnotists, but he soon found out that he had to do with unreliable ones (for had he not read "all the books on hypnosis"!)

"How did you find out that?"

"Very easy. There were a number of fellows in the waiting room, already under hypnosis, and they were lying down fast asleep. I am no fool . . . I ran away at once."

The experienced analyst at once observes that the patient dreads the hypnosis and is afraid of the hypnotizer. The patient assumes that he would like to be hypnotized, but always finds some reason to keep away from the hypnotist.

I point out to the man that he probably does not want to be hypnotized at all. He has already read every book on hypnosis, not for information, however, but to protect himself against the hypnotist.

"This much I can tell you right off . . ." calls out the patient. "You can never suggest to me something that goes against my grain. It is my one fear. You might suggest something that would be unpleasant to me or that might be dangerous."

"And what could that be?"

"For instance, some sexual deed, which might be against my nature. . . ."

"What sort of an act? Explain yourself frankly."

"A homosexual deed."

Then I knew why the patient sought hypnosis and at the same time was afraid of it. He craved a homosexual act. But it should take place during hypnosis, on the gratification-without-guilt principle (*Lust ohne Schuld! Stekel*). On the other hand he was afraid of it. He was under the dominion of two clashing psychic tendencies.

Regarding his history: he was always a hypochondriac concerning his bowels. This very preoccupation with the anal region already shows that the anus played an important rôle in his erogeneity. Has masturbated for a long time. Cannot remember at what age he began. At 20 years of age he began to have intercourse with women, and at 40 he had the misfortune of acquiring a gonorrhœal infection which proved refractory to treatment. The saying that "gonorrhœa is the touchstone for a weak brain" proved true in his case. He grew seriously ill and acquired all sorts of anxiety thoughts. He always anticipated complications, and kept running to doctors insisting that something be done for him. Finally the gonorrhœa was cured but the nervous symptoms persisted, particularly the vague anxieties, the palpitation and the sleeplessness. Then he heard of a famous specialist who discovered an inflammation of the prostate and who gave him massage treatments for about three months.

During the treatment he got along splendidly. His troubles were over and he regained good health. The anxiety feelings were gone and he could not say enough in praise of his physician. He would have liked to have kept up the treatment endlessly. But one day the doctor told him that he was cured, and that he did not need the massage treatments any longer. That did not particularly please him. And in a short time new symptoms arose compelling him to go again to that specialist. The latter examined him anew, declared that the prostate was entirely well and believing the symptoms to be purely nervous he referred the patient to a nerve specialist. He did not like the new specialist and preferred to go without treatment. But soon thereafter, within a few weeks, the old fear of open places reasserted itself so that he could not leave his house at all, unless a friend accompanied him, as when compelled to visit the famous hypnotist.

The development of the agoraphobia is to be explained as follows: the prostatic massage yielded a certain measure of gratification to his anal-erotic trends thus bringing about an improvement in his condition. With the termination of the treatment, the sudden abstinence made his condition worse. His fear of the street was the fear of a homosexual assault, which he also craved at the same time. Thus his dread amounted to an insurance against his homosexual cravings.

It should be mentioned also that the patient carried on anal masturbation through the insertion of an oiled glass tube. Sexual intercourse produced but mild orgasm, whereas during anal masturbation his orgasm was very strong.

The prostatic massage, consequently, was but a repetition of his unconquered masturbation trend and could not but awaken the longing after infantile forms of gratification. He was one of those persons who cannot get along without the enema tube. Whenever his symptoms became particularly troublesome he had recourse to enemas. That was his cryptic form of masturbation. After this procedure he always felt pleasantly refreshed and stimulated.

Through hypnosis he expected to overcome his opposition to the homosexual act. He hoped through that means to experience once again what the prostatic massage had yielded him in the form of pleasurable relief. He meant the therapeutist to gratify also his sexual need.

He relates a typical dream:

I am on the street. I notice that somebody is following me from behind. I run ahead very excitedly. It may be a robber. I feel a sharp sword touching me from behind and I wake up with dread.

Analysis of this dream is superfluous. The sword is a phallic symbol.

I have already mentioned that the erotic stimulation through a physician's therapeutic manipulations leaves out of the situation the feeling of guilt which is otherwise intimately linked with every auto-erotic act. The problem of masturbation cannot be solved unless we understand the genesis of this feeling of guilt.

Before proceeding to the analysis of the masturbator's feeling of guilt, we must point out another important feature. Masturbation is always a regression (*Freud*) back to the level of infantile sensuality. It even replaces the first and the strongest gratification known to man: the pleasure of sucking. I have repeatedly found among masturbators the phantasy that the penis stands for the nipple that is being milked. Masturbation among men is frequently called milking. In my work, *The Language of Dreams*,[3b] will be found a sufficient number of masturbation and sucking dreams to prove this contention.

These facts are enough to show that giving up the masturbation habit is something that certain

[3b] Authorized English version by *James S. Van Teslaar.*

persons must find impossible. Others, of course,
abandon the habit without much trouble. They are
the ones who masturbate while dwelling in their
phantasy on "normal" sexual intercourse,—if I may
use this term for the sake of clarity. For the latter
masturbation serves as a stepping stone towards the
attainable, before it is actually attained.

Persons of this type usually display but little of
the feeling of guilt that plays such a tremendous
rôle in the lives of the other masturbators.

That leads us to remarkable surprises. Patients
come to us exhibiting bitter remorse on account of
masturbation. The matter is explained to them and
they are told: moderate indulgence is harmless. But
they remain incredulous,—in spite of everything,
their feelings of self-reproach persist. We may
understand this occurrence once we know that the
patient's reproaches belong to the phantasies accompanying his indulgence. In the course of the analysis we uncover the various phantasies and note that
the reproaches still persist. Finally we discover that
a shifting of the affects has taken place: *Masturbation has taken over a series of reproaches, unknown
to consciousness, because they are even much more
painful than the reproaches against masturbation.
The masturbation habit becomes a culture medium
for all feelings of remorse. It stands forth, to a
certain extent, as the symbol of all guilt.*

The masturbation habit is tolerated very well by

some persons and not at all by others, depending
entirely on whether the habit is linked with a feeling
of guilt or not. When the sense of guilt accompa-
nies the act, we find all the symptoms ordinarily
ascribed to the habit. If the thought of remorse is
absent, the subject is free of neurotic symptoms.

It is extremely important to recognize this shifting
of the sense of remorse or feeling of guilt. It is an
occurrence we have repeatedly the opportunity of
observing any day in our practice. The patients
admit having masturbated. But the last time it was
three years or more ago, etc. Later we discover
that the last auto-erotic act was carried out but a
few days previously. Patients behave in the same
manner about gonorrhœa. They are inclined to
shift far back the causative incident.

The principle of time displacement plays a tremendous rôle in the development of the compulsion
neuroses. Here is one example among many I could
quote: A woman reproaches herself for an abortion
dating 20 years back. For twenty years she lived in
peace and happiness when suddenly the old occurrence comes to her mind and makes her miserable,
robbing her of her sleep. Moreover, the abortion
had been performed upon the advice of her family
physician. Analysis discloses that she broke down
in health after her husband's illness. One might
think that was due to the self-sacrificing cares of

nursing him and to worry. On the contrary, during the unloved husband's illness the criminal thought came to her: *"O! if he should only die, I would be free and inherit everything!"* The wish was suppressed. But the affect searched out a point through which it might press into consciousness. The feeling of remorse would not be downed! It compelled her to scrutinize her past. Has she not committed once murder? Is not abortion infanticide? And were not the death wishes against the husband an equivalent for murder? An eye for an eye! The feeling of guilt, which arose in connection with a recent event, thus linked itself to an occurrence which had been almost forgotten, filling her with new affects.

Persons who have indulged in masturbation do likewise. They look back searching for some incident to which they may link their current feeling of guilt. Masturbation lends itself most fittingly to serve such a purpose. Indeed, *no other habit reflects so plainly before our eyes the whole struggle between instinct and repression. Masturbation becomes the symbol of our whole struggle between instinct and repression.*[4] *It stands forth as the quintessence of everything forbidden and sinful.*

---

[4] The patients tell us the precise conditions if we but know how to understand them. For instance, a woman suffering from compulsion neurosis who had the fancy of doing away with her father and her mother, told me, after an auto-erotic indulgence: *"Yesterday* I have masturbated again for the first

That is the reason why all the teachings about the harmless character of auto-erotic indulgences have no effect. The reproaches have another origin and can be dealt with only after being traced to their true source.

Teleological thinking is a widespread defect of the intellect and one not easily corrected. Religion is harnessing sex, exploiting it for its own uses. Indulgence in sex is conceived as sinful unless it serve the higher purpose of race propagation. In this teleologic sense masturbation is a purposeless squandering of something useful. Sterile intercourse at least imitates the religiously sanctioned sexual act

time in ten years. Now I have a horrible dread. I now feel that I am about to give way to my murderous inclination since I have not been able to control myself over *the matter of masturbating.*

Before the analysis this patient could not get along and was unable to work at all. All day long she struggled against the murder impulses. She was no longer able to leave the room and never went alone on the street. Now she is self-reliant and working in an office, where she must keep busy the whole day. As was shown by the analysis of her dreams, she has masturbated all along in the night. But she knew nothing about her masturbation indulgence and she thus escaped any self-reproaches on that account. As soon as she got well she began masturbating now and then through the day. A portion of her phantasies again bobbed up into consciousness.

In the course of the analysis I did not concern myself at all with the masturbation. I merely explained to her that the masturbation habit was not harmful and that her sense of guilt must have other reasons. This patient had achieved a certain sense of reassurance through her control over the habit: *"So long as you do not masturbate you will not kill!"* After the analysis enabled her to look upon her murder notions as a harmless indulgence of her over-heated phantasy and in consequence she had no longer any reason to fear herself she was able to indulge "consciously" in masturbation.

leading to increase. Masturbation, on the other hand, is asocial,—it conflicts with the modern conscience. Man cannot rid himself of the questions: whither? what for? That is the teleological determinant of the guilty conscience.

On the other hand the guilty conscience fulfills an important function as a means for enhancing the gratification. Every pleasure involves the principle of its own enhancement. But through repetition the sense of gratification tends to grow pale. This leads to a change of pleasurable objectives or to an increase of stimulus. Masturbation hardly lends itself to a quantitative increase of stimulus. *Rank,* in his study, *The Artist,* was the first to point out that "we have the tendency of increasing our sense of gratification through the development of inner resistances." Anything that we may attain with ease loses its charm for us. We always seek the eternal struggle. In fact, we are innate fighters, combat is a necessity for us. Current social conditions preclude formal physical combat so we resort to the staging of inner conflicts. We generate artificial resistances for the pleasure-gratification of overcoming them and thereby we enhance also the pleasure-value of the victory.

Masturbation owes its highest pleasure-value to the fact that it is something forbidden.[5]

[5] It does not seem man's fate to endure pleasure without experiencing inhibition. It is erroneous to believe that the Catho-

*The masturbator's guilty conscience is a handy
cloak as well as a stimulating factor. In that connection, too, we observe the operation of the principle which I have called the "bipolarity of all
psychic phenomena." The inhibition proves a stimulant and at the same time the stimulant acts as an
inhibition.*

Every act of masturbation becomes a competi-
tive struggle enhancing the zest of achievement.
Too rapid depreciation of the act is guarded against
by the subjective imposition of certain limits to the
indulgence. The guilty conscience thus functions
automatically in a double sense: it heightens the
sense of gratification and at the same time protects
against the depreciation which might result through
excess.

Considering the complicated bearings of masturbation as an incubation medium for all feelings of
guilt, and the feelings of guilt themselves as a stimulant, we may easily appreciate that a mere explanation of the harmless character of the habit will fail
to reassure a patient who suffers from the dread of
the consequences of the habit. We may achieve, at
best, a transitory peace of mind, as in the case of the
hypochondriac who is reassured by the physician

lic church had devised the notion of guilt, by decreeing sexual
intercourse as sinful. Here cause and effect are transposed.
Could that religion have spread had it not corresponded to a
vital need? The human race was horrified at its own pleasure-
seeking.

that there is really nothing the matter with him.
Within a few days, or hours, the old feeling of guilt
reasserts itself, and the patient begins once more to
doubt and to fear: masturbation must be harmful
after all! Books "say so"; his own conscience tells
him, etc.

Very often we may find persons giving up masturbation without any extraneous warning against the
alleged evil consequences of the habit. An inner
voice suddenly tells them: "Do not do this; it is
sinful and very dangerous." Sometimes the old infantile imperatives reassert themselves and seem like
a fresh and new light on the subject. Again it may
be but the dread of indulgence, the fear of pleasure
which always lurks in man's soul. In this connection, too, the guilty feeling generated by another set
of instincts makes itself felt by linking itself to the
practice of masturbation. A voice which also declares: "You do not deserve this indulgence!" *The
secret judgment decreed by man's inner judge strikes
most heavily precisely in the realm where man's
highest gratification awaits him: in connection with
masturbation.*

Such sufferers can be freed of their deeply troubled conscience and of their neuroses only through
analysis, or through complete self-knowledge. Masturbation is but the battle field upon which the
struggle is staged between wish and inhibition, between craving and fear. The habit reminds man

continually of his weakness compelling him to surround himself with defences and protective measures,
with inhibitions and reassurances. But in its turn
the habit is man's best defensive measure against the
outbreak of his paraphilia. So long as he masturbates he abstains from acting out his forbidden
phantasies.

The principles which I have outlined show that an
act, harmless in itself, may be the partial cause of a
neurosis and may also play a great partial rôle in
the dynamics of the neurosis.

I may add a few remarks on the treatment and the
prophylaxis of masturbation. Eventually children
abandon the habit and they require no warnings
from parents. It is ridiculous to attempt to "cure"
children of the habit by circumcision, or with beatings and threats,—measures which only fill the child's
sensitive heart with great dread. We must see to it
that the child is not unnecessarily exposed to excitations during the nursery period, although I am far
from agreeing with *Sadger* that faulty nursery care
alone is responsible for masturbation. It is well
known that dogs and monkeys and other animals also
masturbate and there can be no question of wrong
nursery habits in their case. We must take care
that the child's sensuality is not roused prematurely,
we must have the child busily preoccupied with
healthful games and keep careful watch over his
various auto-erotic manifestations.

In most cases the children abandon spontaneously the habit. Masturbation, obviously, has its significant function. During the nursing period the infant finds an inexhaustible source of pleasure in its nutritional functions. Weaning from the breast amounts to a serious trauma. The child frankly seeks gratification wherever it may be found. After weaning auto-erotic activity is markedly increased.

Only the analyst is capable of forming a correct idea of the deleterious effects upon the human psyche which the struggle against masturbation may bring about, a struggle made more acute by the well-meaning but ignorant doctrines of our professional sex purists and meddling moralists. The taboo against masturbation, as the representative of all social taboos, plays a tremendous rôle in the dynamics of the neuroses. Many severe neuroses are traceable to parental threats. Some of the strange means whereby parents propose to break their children of the habit are astonishing. One father compels his boy to swear on his life that he "won't do it again." Shortly thereafter the boy falls a prey to the temptation; thereupon he feels himself guilty of the great crime of patricide. Another father threatens to castrate the sinner if he "catches him at it again." Another father, as a strong warning against the habit, showed his boy some gruesome pictures of the alleged consequences (insanity, paralysis, spinal trouble, impotence, premature old age, etc.) and

thereafter, through association with the terrible pictures, the act of masturbation became each time a
dreadful ordeal. Such warnings do not always act
as preventives. I have already pointed out that
masturbation may be adopted as a means for carrying out self-destruction, or chronic suicide, through
cutting short one's "life thread." Taboos have never
proven themselves educative determinants. Thou
shalt not!—often the commandment acts as a
stimulus.

Educators should bear in mind also that what is
forbidden becomes thereby enhanced in value as a
stimulant. Taboos increase the pleasure expectation. On the other hand it is much easier to achieve
the desired end by permitting moderate indulgence.
In fact, *I believe that if it were commonly permitted
masturbation would lose most of its charm.*[6]

My procedure with adults is very similar. I explain to them the harmless character of auto-erotism
and leave it to them to decide what their conduct
should be. I endeavor to influence the patients who
confide in me, wherever possible, in favor of the
"normal" act. But without compulsion. Sometimes it works. But not always. Consider, for
instance, the widely prevalent fear of infection.

[6] We observe, for instance, that in Italy, where homosexuality
is not punished, it plays a lesser rôle than in Germany. In
Italy homosexual prostitution caters chiefly to foreigners and
is quite a flourishing business maintained largely for foreigners.

Many men, being very religious, regard extra-marital relations as sinful. For such men masturbation is the one means to keep them active and well until marriage.

Some writers believe that the habit affects sexual potence and is the cause of premature ejaculation. But men suffering from *ejaculatio præcox* disclose some very remarkable facts. Once in a while they come across a woman with whom they are satisfactorily potent. Or, trying some variant, whereby the repressed components of their libido also find an outlet, they find themselves surprisingly potent. Such men are pronounced bisexuals, or paraphiliacs, they suffer from this weakness only because ordinarily they bring into play but a portion of their sexuality.

I quote a single illustration. A man consulted me for *ejaculatio præcox;* he showed distinct signs of a homosexual predisposition, therefore I advised him to try *coitus inversus* as well as other positions. He comes back beaming happiness. His potence was so strong, his wife experienced orgasm twice during the sexual embrace. A knowledge of the "ars amandi" is an important equipment for the conscientious physician. Wonders may be achieved through proper advice. Unfortunately, not always. Among masturbators there are many cryptic homosexuals as well as victims of other paraphilias for whom coitus is not a thoroughly adequate form of sexual gratification; therefore there are naturally among them many who suffer from *ejaculatio præcox*, or psychic impotence.[7]

It is high time to abolish altogether the legend that masturbation is harmful. Physicians are hardly able to see the subject in its true light since they are judge and interested party at the same time. The feeling of guilt accompanying every masturbation affects also the judgment of physicians who, as all other men, must have also once been addicted to the practice. That is why so many untrue and mischievous statements are being upheld with a tone of genuine conviction.

The terrible sufferings caused by the false teachings and warnings can hardly be overestimated. Any one who observes with unbiased mind some of the more serious neuroses brought on by the false teachings of sex alarmists and self-appointed moral purists, cannot but conclude that masturbation is, at least, a lesser evil than the means whereby mischievous meddlers attempt to combat it.

We must change fundamentally our attitude towards the problem of masturbation. There is no "normal" sexual act. Certain forms of sexual gratification are the only adequate ones for certain individuals. In every instance this is sharply delineated

[7] On the relationship between masturbation and *potentia*, vid. my study, *Male Impotence,* authorized English version by *Dr. James S. Van Teslaar.*

and variously determined: through ethical and religious doctrines, or by the laws of the land. There are numberless transitional phases; who dares attempt to determine where the normal ends and the pathological begins?

Masturbation is a return to infantile gratification. It is a symptom of psychic infantilism, characteristic of the neurotic. At the right time the child abandons its childish ways if properly trained to assume the rôle of an adult. But this is not to be achieved through taboos and threats; it is a question of education and of growth through freedom, such as may be attained through psychoanalysis.

Wo nur auf Erden bisher die religiöse Neurose aufgetreten ist, finden wir sie verknüpft mit drei gefährlichen Diätverordnungen: Einsamkeit, Fasten und geschlechtlicher Enthaltsamkeit.

NIETZSCHE

V

Religion the Guardian of Sexuality—Masturbation and the Problem of Fertility—A Case of Religious Neurosis—A Minister's Influence on his Congregation—Glossolalia (Gift of Tongues)—Dementia following Struggle against Masturbation—The Masturbator Himself a God—Sexuality pervades Religion—What a Minister writes about the Dangers of Masturbation—The Mental Hygiene of the Future—A Modern Instance of Mental Hygiene—Marcinowski's New Religion.

V

Wherever the neurosis of religion made its appearance thus far on earth, we find it linked to three terrible prescriptions—solitude, fasting and sexual abstinence.

NIETZSCHE

The masturbator experiences his most serious conflicts whenever religious inhibitions are linked to the others. The fear inspired by the written and oral teachings that the habit ruins health, that it brings on spinal cord trouble, impotence, and early invalidism, or that it destroys one's mental energies is strengthened by this ethical emphasis. The masturbator feels himself in the throes of a vice, he thinks that he has not the right to consider himself a "pure man" and that he commits sin. His religious inhibitions render the struggle more significant, more bitter and difficult. It is not merely a question of earthly welfare, one's hope of salvation is at stake. Thus in fighting the habit the masturbator fights also for the salvation of his soul. Every particular act which furnishes even a passing sense of gratification interferes with the certainty of eternal bliss and seems to lead to damnation. It is certainly a

striking fact that all religions have stood irrecon-
cilably against personal freedom in matters of sex,
with the exception of the Greek religion which has
also furnished us the healthiest people. Every
religion conceives itself to be the guardian of sexuality. It is of the greatest significance that mar-
riages are consummated in the church. Religion does
not permit man to dispose freely of his gratification
sense. He must accept it from the minister's hand
as a gift of God. So-called "free" love has always
been the religion of the atheists and of those whose
ethical formulations stand beyond the proscriptions
of religion.

But masturbation is a practice that obviously
deprives the priestly class of its control over sex.
It is a habit that not only makes the individuals
concerned self-reliant and free but it also tends to
exempt them from every social obligation: it shifts
the sexual instinct itself beyond every teleological
obligation. From the standpoint of the recognized
religion the sexual instinct is but the means for reproduction: "Like the sands of the sea shall you
increase and therefore you must not waste your
seed." This doctrine is traceable back to the
nomadic period, during which the most numerous
tribe was also the strongest. It was the interest of
the priestly class to foster the highest fertility
among its dependents. We note to this day that
among the religious Jews of Russia and Poland all

means for the limitation of conception are scorned as very sinful and even the lowest classes endure willingly all the social consequences of unbridled fertility. Masturbation and homosexuality stood against the interests of the State. It was to the interest of the State to curb these tendencies, inasmuch as increase of numbers was its chief concern. Times have changed. Numbers alone are no longer the chief asset of the State. But that was certainly the case at one stage. And inasmuch as the religions we possess are inheritances from older days and since, moreover, the future of the race does not yet enter vitally into our current considerations and does not materially affect our conduct, we still cling pertinaciously to certain dogmas which were of the very greatest social significance in the past, even though some of these dogmas not only no longer fit our present day but are, in part, actually harmful.

The statement I made above that religion discountenances masturbation altogether I must modify. One current religion is an exception: the Catholic. I shall have opportunity later to discuss a number of cases illustrating the influence of the confessional on the course of the masturbation neurosis. But even evangelic ministers know to influence their dependents, and to bring them out, without the formula of confession. Cases illustrating this fact are at my disposal in large numbers. It is gratifying to note that the ministers are now

beginning to turn their attention to psychology, and
specifically, to psychoanalysis.[1]   The benefit they
may derive thereby is greater than the harm which
certain premature expressions may cause or may
have actually brought about.

Above all, it is desirable that the ministers learn
to appreciate the all-powerfulness of the sexual instinct and to know its manifestations as well as its
various masks.

The next case, which I record below, takes us to
one of the chief cities of Germany.   Nevertheless it
plunges us into the darkness of the medieval period,
and brings before our vision pictures that clearly
do not belong to our age.   The antisexual instinct
—there must be such a trend, otherwise occurrences
such as are about to be recorded would not be possible—corresponds to man's forward urge and discloses his craving for self-reliance.   Man strives to
rise above all earthly and sensual cravings, he wants
to disregard his animal promptings.   He wants to
master his instincts.   That this is not possible with-

---

[1] It would be unfair not to mention in this connection *Dr.
Oskar Pfister,* of Zürich, the first minister who has had the
courage to adopt publicly psychoanalysis.   His important work,
The Psychoanalytic Method (English version by *Payne,* Moffat,
Yard & Co., N. Y.) is one of the most valuable contributions
which have been made towards enlarging and spreading the
new science.   The book, primarily intended for educators, may
be recommended also to all physicians interested in psychoanalysis as an excellent introduction to the subject.

On the educational bearings of the new psychology, *vid.* also:
Dr. James S. Van Teslaar's monograph, *Newer Ideals in Child
Training.*

out serious sacrifice, none knows better than the psychoanalyst who always meets those who are most seriously wounded or crippled in this struggle.

CASE 19. Miss O. Z., school teacher, 28 years of age, has masturbated since childhood and has always been well. She had always been an intelligent, strong child and an excellent pupil. She passed her examinations satisfactorily and began very early to train herself for the earnest calling of an educator of youth. She always lived within the circle of her parents whom she charmed with her lively temperament and her healthy humor. She never troubled her mind over masturbation, though she indulged almost daily in the habit. She was very clear-minded and said to herself: "I do not know whether I shall ever marry; who wants a poor school teacher nowadays for a wife!" She was not particularly attractive,—rather slim and thin, squint-eyed, and her skin texture poor. She did not care much for men and instead kept up a close friendship with some of her women colleagues. She masturbated apparently without any particular fantasy merely in response to an unbearable excitation, which disappeared after the indulgence, so that she slept quietly afterwards.

Suddenly she returned to Vienna. Her mother brought her back seriously ill. She began to have sudden spells during which her sense of awareness

left her completely, but afterwards she could recall
no trace of these episodes of absent-mindedness.
During the spells she indulged in masturbation
openly and without shame, at the same time uttering
words which horrified those around her who knew
her as a woman of retired and chaste disposition.
But let us record the experience in the patient's
own words:

I want to relate to you with utmost candor and
regard for the truth how my spells began. I was
always a healthy-minded girl, now and then a little
dreamy and romantic, with a slight disposition to
building castles in the air,—but on the whole always
active and very energetic. You know already that
I have masturbated since childhood. Now I want
to tell you how my mind turned against the habit
and what terrible consequences this change in attitude brought upon me.

Some time ago I lived in one of the larger ladies'
boarding houses. There was a very strict churchly-
Christian atmosphere about the place due, chiefly,
to another boarder and enhanced by the friendly
relations of the house with an Evangelic-Lutheran
minister. That atmosphere was entirely new and
foreign to me. Neither in my parental home nor
among my friends had I ever met such persons as
those in whose midst I now found myself day by
day. I became friendly with a couple of young

ladies—both older than I—and soon we grew very
fond of one another. The invitation to join the
minister's services and Bible study class I accepted
partly through courtesy and partly out of curiosity,
though I frankly showed before everybody my own
disposition which was free and wholly different.
But soon I was charmed by the minister's words,
and the whole theme of religion appealed to me in
a new light. I dwelled devotedly on my new feelings. The beauty and nobility of the Christian religion so appealed to me that I now felt the wish to
be able to believe,—and to be as clean and pure,—
as my women friends. I resolved to give up masturbation. This I did secretly. To my friends I
spoke merely of the religious upheaval and change
that was going on within me. My friends as well
as the minister supported me, trying to dispel my
doubts. They endeavored over and over to convert
my emotional attachment to religion into an open
confession of faith, though mere emotional allegiance
seemed more compatible with my nature. For some
time I felt fairly comfortable within that environment.

I may mention that I found myself in that environment at a period in my life when I was particularly sensitive to new impressions, such impressions having, I might say, a soothing effect upon me.
Masturbation I had learned in childhood,—a girl
friend taught me. I had indulged in the habit

almost every night before falling asleep. Now, under
the influence of the religious environment, I gave up
the habit,—after a long, hard struggle. Religiosity seemed to me a rich substitute, the thought of
being "pure" upheld me. But I slept poorly and
lived practically in a continuous state of ecstasy.
This state, quite naturally, affected me, and often
distressingly. For a time I succeeded in banishing
the thought of masturbation as well as my erotic
phantasies, but only for a time. Physical activity
might have induced a healthy fatigue, but my work
was mental, and that, instead of fostering sleep,
made for sleeplessness. I grew nervous, irritable,
restless. The woman friend who watched over me
lovingly, questioned me about the reason for my
irritability and restlessness. I did not think it necessary to tell any one (even though it be my very
closest friend) anything about my painful struggles
and my sensual temptations, holding the conviction
that these things are best borne alone. But she
pressed me again and again, insisting that she could
certainly help me. Mental overwork had made me
extremely nervous at the time and now my irritability grew; I felt worse and worse, certain of my
friend's remarks made me think that she surmised,—
and condemned,—everything, anyway,—so I made
a clean breast of it all, *i. e.*, she asked me questions
and I answered them, her questions causing me to
appraise myself quite differently, of course, than I

would have done without my friend's coöperation. She branded my restlessness as sinful excitation against which I must fight with spiritual weapons. She urged upon me most pressingly the need of avoiding every thought that might swerve me off the path upon which alone, she thought, I could find peace. She wanted me to break up altogether my friendship with a young woman who influenced me in a direction quite the reverse of hers. That was a young artist, a very intelligent girl, whose range of untrammelled thinking had not affected me unsympathetically theretofore and who, above all, had at no time seemed to me either bad or particularly sinful. I was extremely roused to see all that branded as sinful. I could not conscientiously admit the need of breaking with my dear friend, the young artist woman. Abandon all memories, give up all external reminiscences of my youth, fight "with spiritual weapons" against every sensual temptation —I could not bring myself to do it! Yet I was asked to do all that by a being who, on account of her quiet self-assurance, her earnest goodness and her love for me, had a tremendous influence on me, a woman who, moreover, was fully aware of the influence she thus exercised upon me. I felt that she was doing it with the best of intentions—but I could not acquiesce in the thought that everything was sinful. Not only must I break that friendship, I was to do so joyfully,—Christ requires joyful obedience,—"the sacrifice of the most beloved is the gate to the kingdom of God."

Indeed, that was something I could not do. And over and over again that terrible admonition: *you must!* The fatal: *either—or!* Either Christ or Satan! Abandon everything, everything,—or there's no help!

At about that time I had to take examinations in a couple of foreign languages. The trouble came on top of it all! My friend comforted me day by day in every possible way, but even during the critical time she held before me, over and over, the thought that my faith must keep growing through the curbing of my desires, that everything else was but secondary. I grew so extremely nervous that I had repeated dizziness and fainting spells so that at the time of the examinations I was hardly able to sit up. I was nearly in despair and by that time I actually imagined that my thoughts and my feelings were thoroughly sinful. I struggled on in the midst of my despair. I had but one wish: peace! That was what I was promised. But instead of becoming more calm, I grew more and more irritable. I spoke to my old friend again, begging her to permit me the forbidden friendship—but I felt torture even as I did so. And then again fear and restlessness, inasmuch as my failure to break quickly and "joyfully" with the old relations was pointed out to me as in itself sinful. And that was something

I could not bear! My woman friend tried to quiet me down, and in fact she succeeded in helping me over some distressing hours with her quiet talk and our joint prayer. But when I was alone, especially at night, the old dread seized me: what will become of me! And all along I had a notion that I deserved all this, that the struggle will do me good and must finally lead me to victory. I was extremely irritable and at the same time so very tired! I had reached the end of my strength—I was so far gone physically as well as mentally that something had to happen. Peace is what I had to have; but when I needed it most, I was not granted that boon. I reached the feeling that this was even physically the end of me and I gave my letters, pictures and diaries to my friend, all the mementoes of our friendship, to be destroyed. It was hard to part from everything! She burned everything in my presence. It broke me to pieces.

About the nights and days immediately following I recall nothing clearly. At any rate, my unrest reached its highest summit at night. I then acted as one bereft of senses, crying, shouting, throwing myself around in bed and speaking out everything that had so terribly oppressed my heart for weeks and months. Of all that I have no recollection, except that I remember the general feeling I then had: a feeling of something indescribable within me compelling me to speak out—I had to talk things out without, and even against, my will. *What I said I do not know.* A physician was called—he was wholly a stranger to me—and he advised: leave her alone! The minister was also called, the one who had such a strong influence upon my woman friend. Everything that my friend had said and done had been entirely in concordance with the minister's view—even though I believe it was not done with his direct knowledge. Now my friend thought the time had come to tell him everything: about my struggles, my temptations, my doubts. I myself should have never taken the minister into my confidence regarding these matters, even though I had great faith in his admirable qualities as man and as spiritual adviser. He now found out everything and took the whole matter in his hands. But that I learned only afterwards.

After the excitement I became quiet, very quiet; the reaction was complete. I imagined it was all over and I rejoiced so much over my bit of freedom! With the others I went to the Bible class. The minister spoke on Romans 8.6: "For to be carnal minded is death; but to be spiritually minded is life and peace."

The whole preachment, an earnest admonition to repent, applied to me. I well noted that fact, while strangers may have not known it. My whole painfully subdued restlessness began all over when I saw the whole course of my doing, thinking and feeling thus publicly pilloried as bad, abominable and deadly.

Thus far my two women friends had been kind and touchingly sympathetic towards me. They had tried to help me insofar as it was in their power. I felt deeply grateful to them; their true friendship had been a real comfort to me.

One day, it was after a Bible class meeting, my two friends suddenly called on me: "Our love, our confidence, our friendship is at an end, so far as you are concerned. We don't even feel pity for you any longer. Your nightly tantrums were a sham. You are a wicked, wicked person, a sensuous creature through and through; you have abandoned yourself to most horrible passions. You are unsound at the bottom of your heart. Do not try to win us back, you won't succeed. Either you or we leave the house! We won't be under the same roof with you! So,—and now we have nothing more to say to you!"

I must confess that at first these words did not affect me too deeply. I went quietly back to bed— I had been called out of sleep at a late hour to be told these things. But later on despair again seized me. That they should do such a thing to me, —when everything with which they reproached me was untrue! Should they have done it? Was I, after all, so bad that I had to be avoided—that they had to wound me to such an extent? Had I not

sacrificed the friendship of my artist friend, had I
not given up the masturbation habit after super-
human struggles against it? Why should I be held
responsible for my unfortunate spells? I had no
knowledge of what I had been saying during those
terrible spells and that is something I do not know
to this day. The depths of my despair no one can
perceive.

How I got along during the days immediately
following I do not know; I only recall that every
thought seemed tender and painful and the everlasting, despairing cry: why? They have been so good
to me! I haven't done anything.

My parents, advised by others of my plight, immediately called me back home. My two friends
avoided the least word with me. Once more I went
to see the minister. He reproached me for my wick-
edness, branded my nightly spells as nothing less
than "satanic," and he so shook up and scared me
that I found myself too weak to say anything in
self-defence. He almost convinced me that I was as
wicked as he made me out, that I deserved everything
—I believe I would have been willing to acknowledge myself guilty of all the crimes of which I had
been wholly ignorant till then—only to find some
reasonable excuse for the harsh and cruel conduct of
my friends, of whom I had thought so much. The
minister promised he might help me some time in

the future. I thanked him for everything and believed everything he said.

I was told they would continue to pray for me—how long they might find this still possible no one could tell. But help me in any other way they could no longer: "We no longer feel ourselves called upon to be your saviour!" Plainly, I was thrown out of the fold, abandoned to my fate as hopeless.

With deepest despair gripping my heart, the eternal *why?* staring me in the face, I left for home. Back home the first few weeks were perhaps the hardest; all external stimuli subdued, I became the more helplessly a prey to the inner unrest. Nothing seemed worth while, nothing roused any interest in me. Always the one thought: "If you are as bad as that, what is going to be the end?" And again: "Why have they done that to you?"

My parents were baffled. And, after repeated pressing questions and inquiries on their part the truth finally came out. The minister wrote that it was he who had advised the two women friends to break with me. And the reason? He felt that my love for them was something perverse. From the fact that the .physician's order was, "leave her alone!" and because the friend had told him that it quieted me during my worst spells for her to take me lovingly into her arms, the minister formed and hurled against me a most horrible accusation. **My**

friend herself had never observed any such unnatural
feeling in me.   At first the two friends were not of
the minister's opinion (what the second friend had
to do with it I do not quite understand), but finally
they agreed with him.   Without the least substantial
reason they felt themselves justified to talk to me
as I have related above, to drive me out of the
house—to let me slink back home broken in spirit
and a prey to despair.   Without telling the truth!
I asked for proofs; my parents requested the minister to forward some evidence justifying that suspicion which had resulted in such serious consequences for me.   Not a word!   Instead his letter contained the threat that he would report me to the
school authorities should my parents try to affect
his standing.

It did not improve my condition in the least to
become acquainted with the contents of that letter.
That with which they now reproached me was, again,
something entirely new, and I had never heard of it
before.

Along with my self-reproaches there arose now
within me reproaches against others.   And above
and beyond it all, there was the eternal can't-under-
stand-it feeling, and the oppressive *"why?"*   Not a
minute passed, day or night, that I did not think of
this trouble.   I do not know what might become of
me had my parents not taken me to a physician, who
saved me, in spite of the minister's contention that

only a "spiritual adviser" could be of any help in my case.

That is a XXth Century occurrence in the midst of a so-called highly cultured circle. We thus see that the age of exorcism has not yet passed; the devil is still plying his abominable trade.

I was called to see the patient during a spell. She was in the midst of a typical hysteric attack and threw herself convulsively around. She uttered meaningless words; occasionally in the midst of her glossolalia [2] one made out such expressions as "beloved," "bliss," "delight," etc. Then she stuck her finger into the anus with short, sharp, boring motions, the ordeal ending in an orgasm, during which her face assumed an ecstatic, transfigured expression. Apparently she played the rôle of a man overpowering a woman *a posteriori*.

That was during the beginning of the treatment. But under the influence of the analysis, her usual self soon reasserted itself and all morbid manifestations disappeared. She was again able to sleep and had no further spells. To this day—eight years after the treatment—I receive occasionally a letter from her. She is entirely well, and has resumed relations with her earlier, free-minded friend.

[2] *Dr. Oskar Pfister* has given us an exhaustive account of religious glossolalia (gift-of-tongues) in his study entitled, *Die psychologische Enträtslung der religiösen Glossolalie und der automatischen Kryptographie.* Jahrb. f. psychoanalytische Forschungen. Vol. III, Verlag, Deuticke, Wien und Berlin, 1912.

She had already formerly indulged in masturbation with homosexual phantasies while under half-conscious states. But she knew nothing of homosexuality and did not even suspect that such relations were possible between two women. She became aware of the character of her friendly relations only through the minister, at first, and later, through my explanations. She learned to recognize the human character of these instinctive inclinations and thereupon it was an easy matter for her to overcome them. She wrote me also that she indulges in the old habit again at rare intervals, and that she always feels better after that. Later she married, became a mother, and for a time wrote me no more. I had occasion incidentally of speaking to her and of thus convincing myself that she had found the true path of peace at last. . . .

This case is of particular interest to us because it shows once more that a person tolerating the habit without any evil effects becomes neurotic through suddenly imposed abstinence and is compelled to express the sexual urge through a "spell" of some kind or other. In this instance we find religious and erotic determinants flowing together. The woman's relations with her women friends show distinctly a homosexual root . . . on the part of the latter as well. It was jealousy that prompted them to demand that the woman sacrifice her older friendship. Finally these women identified themselves with one another through their common admiration for the minister, and admiration which was not without its erotic component. The rapid recovery is as noteworthy as the overcoming of the "spell" of religiosity, a transitory development which marked but a temporary regression to an infantile mental attitude.

The next case presents simpler aspects but a more difficult therapeutic problem.

CASE 20. Mr. T. I., a jurist, 24 years of age, finds himself unable to keep up his studies on account of serious depressions. He stays mostly at home, staring absent-mindedly, immersed in day dreams, hardly taking part in conversation, his whole behavior approaching that of a demented individual. He sleeps a great deal and very soundly, lingers in bed mornings, feels tired and crushed, and when he speaks out tortures his family with the admonition that he will not live long. It is hard to manage him as he can hardly be induced to talk. Finally I overcome his inhibitions and I hear the following account of his life history. He was always a quiet child, but stubborn, quick to anger and moody. At six years of age he began to masturbate, without being taught by anybody. He discovered the habit for himself and indulged in it freely during childhood. He kept up the habit to his 16th year, without any after effects; was a good scholar, and physically he also developed very well. Then he began to be influenced by the talk among his fellow pupils. He heard a great deal about masturbation without knowing precisely what was meant. He heard that it was very dangerous, that the habit makes one stupid and that it surely brings on spinal trouble. He asked definite questions concerning the meaning of masturbation and was horrified to hear that it meant self-gratification, the habit in which he had indulged so long. He tried to control himself but found it very difficult to do so. All he succeeded in accomplishing was to indulge at rarer intervals than theretofore. He was always a very religious boy and kept up his religious piety all through the high school years. Therefore he confessed his habit and now he heard that it was also a terrible sin. He promised his spiritual adviser never to indulge again. He kept his promise for three months. Then he was again tempted. Thereupon he realized plainly that he had committed a great sin, which he must atone for, if he was not to be deprived of salvation. Properly to expiate he decided to become a monk and to enter a monastery. But his father would not hear of it and did not grant him permission to do so. Therefore he decided on another means. He expiated by fasting, withdrew from all earthly pleasures and gave up masturbation altogether. But he could not achieve mastery over his sexual promptings. In order to keep from the old habit and preserve his health he began to visit prostitutes. It scared him tremendously when he heard upon confession that he had committed a greater sin, having but jumped from the frying pan into the fire. According to the teachings of religion he must keep himself pure. He thereupon imposed complete abstinence upon himself, endeavouring to smother sensuous thoughts through excessive devotion to his tasks.

In fact he ceased to think of sexual matters and was also no longer troubled by temptations. But how radically his disposition changed! He could neither study nor concentrate his mind on anything. No conclusion seemed to him more obvious than that he had ruined himself through the old indulgence and that he was now but suffering from the early signs of an oncoming mental breakdown! He gave up any further efforts at studying and began to figure how much longer he might last before landing in an insane asylum. What was the use of studying and striving, when a horrible fate already hovered over him and the inevitable was not to be avoided? From day to day he grew more thoughtful and depressed. He gave up all earthly pleasures and awaited the fatal stroke. . . .

In such cases the dread becomes a morbid determinant and in itself generates the very troubles that are feared. Thus the subject assumed the rôle of the insane person he thought he was becoming and begged his father to intern him at the Steinholf, the well known institution for the insane of lower Austria.

The analysis of this patient proceeded piecemeal. He is a shut-in type of person, resolved not to tell everything. Such patients sit for hours before their analyst not knowing what to say. Then want the consultant to ask them questions. They do not dare freely to disclose the flow of their ideas.

The patient tells haltingly about his fears. He is already suffering from the effects of the habit and he will surely land in the institution for the insane. Next he confesses having already attempted suicide twice. We know the relationship between suicide and masturbation. This case brings further proof. Once he wanted to throw himself out of the window. His brother happened to be in the room and saved him in time. Noteworthy is the trivial character of this attempt. It was more a play with the thought of suicide than an attempt. Had he seriously intended to take his life he would not have made the attempt in his brother's presence.

His second attempt at suicide was staged in the presence of his brother-in-law. The latter had once asked him, during a period of marked depression, whether he masturbates, hence the influence that the brother-in-law exercised over him. Having admitted the habit the subject was warned by his brother-in-law against the evil consequences of the indulgence and urged to seek intercourse with women. He was going to shoot his brains before his brother-in-law, but this intention also miscarried. It is noteworthy that all his efforts at self-destruction were directed against the brain—the seat of all thoughts of temptation, the organ that harbors the fear of insanity. He wants to sacrifice the enemy along with his life.

Two dreams obtained during the first few days are interesting. The first is as follows:

My friend K. is in the theatre, where a play I don't know is being given. He makes fun of the author and leaves the theatre talking loudly.

This dream, like all first dreams in the course of an analysis, is the one which portrays the subject's relation to the analyst. The latter is friend K., and the theatre is the analysis. He does not want to stay in it; he argues over the treatment and wants to give up the analysis. Obviously because the "piece" to be given is not to his liking,—because he wants to keep his secrets to himself.

The second dream, however, brings us a little more close to an understanding of the relationship between the neurosis and the masturbation habit.

I dream I am in bed lying on my abdomen and some one I do not know belabors me with a cane.

It does not particularly hurt and that makes me
wonder very much.

"A stupid dream, it means nothing," the subject
adds by way of criticism. Such remarks disclose
resistance and are an attempt at depreciating valuable data; ridicule, of course, is particularly well
adapted to such ends.

But we are justified to surmise masochistic
trends. The subject now tells us that when he was
a child he was often beaten by his father. He was
punished even on account of trifles; his father was
a very strict man. Once he was beaten because his
school report was not satisfactory. . . . These corporeal punishments were apparently never associated
with any pleasurable feeling. He denies any
masochistic phantasies or any trace of a masochistic
disposition.

Any one who has never analyzed a patient determined to withhold something of importance is hardly
able to appreciate the difficulties of analysis. The
subject comes day by day, sits in front of the
analyst, and waits to be asked questions. Indeed,
many physicians have precisely this childish notion
about psychoanalysis. They talk about a painful
third degree, through which the subject is supposed
to be dragged. Such inquisitorial ordeals and third
degree tactics are nonsensical. What the subject
does not give up spontaneously is usually without

value, though it be forced out of him and though
it be significant enough in itself. The subject must
understand that analysis is a process of clarifying
his own soul and that he hurts himself whenever he
lies to the analyst or tries to hide important
facts. . . .

That is the case with this patient. He shows
signs of a terrific inner struggle and admits that
there are things he cannot bring himself to talk
about, though he would like to do so.

He tells me of a strange nocturnal scene, which I
have recorded at length in my *Nervous Anxiety
States*. He is afraid of · heart failure. Almost
every night he has a heart spell and alarms the
whole household. He begins to gasp and his hands
move anxiously over his heart region. His father
comes and reassuring words quiet him a little. Then
his married sister appears on the scene; she pats him
as one does a child and applies compresses over his
poor heart. Thereupon he quiets down like a good
little child and falls asleep.

We are acquainted with the psychogenesis of such
nocturnal spells through the analysis of neurotic
children. Such nightly attacks, of whatever nature,
express the craving and longing for love. The sister
rushes in with but a nightgown over her, and so
does the father; the patient is the center of the
family's attention. He conjures and summons into
his presence the beloved objectives around which his

secret thoughts spin all sorts of phantasies. The
character of these phantasies is something we can
only surmise; we shall know that definitely only
when the patient overcomes his inner resistance
enough to disclose further details. Only then will
we be able to understand his struggle against masturbation and the accompanying feeling of guilt.

Slowly the picture unravels. The attitude towards the father is further illumined. It was at
first vain love and devotion, now hatred rears its
head and throws its shadow across the field of analysis. The father was very strict. He was undoubtedly very kind, perhaps too kind, but he could
also be very strict and then he was unmercifully so.
Because of an unsatisfactory school report he was
once beaten. His father always expected him to
bring home the highest marks on his school record
card. If he slipped down a little ways he was certain to be punished for it. He suffered corporeal
punishment at 16 years of age because he once took
part in a rather lengthy excursion without having
first asked and obtained his father's permission. He
ran away after that and for two days he was not
to be found. Finally he was discovered in the woods
and brought home. After that his father did not
speak a word to him for a whole month. That was
his father's most serious punishment. If he was
angry with the children, he broke all conversation
with them. For a long time the patient was like-

wise practically speechless during the analysis. A tremendous stubbornness dominates him and makes it impossible for him to speak out. He copies his father who had thus punished him and on whom he now revenges himself through his illness. In his fits of depression he is likewise taciturn at home, sitting for weeks at a time dumb-like and brooding in a corner, wholly shut in. His depression and his inability to work are a punishment for the beatings his father gave him, experiences that he has not forgotten to this day. It is not yet possible to determine whether these beatings also proved pleasurable and whether he unconsciously awaits their repetition. He dreams repeatedly of being beaten.

In the midst of endless resistances he confesses one day that he is a masochist and that his onanistic phantasies always revolve around the act of being beaten. The meaning of this emotional attitude, or predisposition, is a theme that will be taken up at length in my volume in the present series dealing with *Masochism*. At this juncture I want merely to point out its relationship to masturbation. It developed further that the patient is emotionally fixed on his family. He loves his father, his brother, and his brother-in-law, and all have been drawn into his homosexual phantasies of being beaten. Finally there is also disclosed an incestuous fixation upon the sister. The patient's remorse derives its strongest affect from these sources. His reproaches are not due to the masturbation habit, in reality they are directed against his incest phantasies. Like all persons who are fixed emotionally upon members of their own family, he runs away and continually tries to break the family bonds, but in vain. His neurosis plunges him more and more into the net of his attachment to the family, he grows more and more unable to meet life self-reliantly, so that he finally becomes like a child living on the father's bounty. The flaring up of the temporarily suspended infantilism reawakens also the criminal trends. Homicidal phantasies are far from rare, and through the operation of the spiritual, *lex talionis*, these bring about thoughts of suicide.

He was unable to attain what he expected from religion: liberation from his morbid instincts and complete freedom. He expected of God what he was unable to achieve for himself. Thereafter for a time he assumed a contrary attitude towards religion, and he passed through a period during which he uttered all sorts of blasphemies, at the same time keeping an atheistic diary, into which he entered daily proofs of the non-existence of God. Those proofs must have had but little convincing power; for he soon reverted to his infantile piety, began to repeat the childhood prayers, adopted "free-will" resolutions for himself, and subjected himself to strict mortifications of the flesh.

But the great sacrifice that he resolved to impose

on himself was the giving up of the habit of masturbation. After giving up this conscious form of
auto-erotic gratification, to be sure, he experienced
pollutions. But he did not think of these occurrences as sinful. He had not "unchastily touched"
himself. He was again pious and ready to give himself over to religion. At twilight he ran to church,
knelt worshipfully, and prayed to be saved and to
be forgiven for his sins. He was in the habit of
repeating the pater noster innumerable times at
night so as to avoid impure thoughts and quiet
down. He plunged into a romantic Mariolatry,
this worship of Mary, incidentally, becoming a
little clearer when we know that his sister's name
was also Mary and that his phantasy pictures of
Mary resembled her. Thus sexuality riled up the
true waters of his faith and mixed in his prayers.
He wanted to achieve purity at all costs, and was
willing to sacrifice even the highest good he possessed,
his life. He gave up studying and no longer concerned himself with the everyday duties inasmuch
as he felt a higher "call." He did not want to lose
his eternal life. He wanted to taste the joys of
salvation.

During the twilight states of his consciousness he
dwelt in that mixed realm of religiosity and erotism
which only ascetes know well. He experienced
ecstasies during which he felt himself pervaded by
blissful feelings. No conscious thought intended

to remind him that he had transposed his libido into religious feelings and that he now was, according to the old standards, doubly guilty. Only inwardly he surmised and did somehow sense the relationship between his libido and his religiosity. He plunged more deeply into illness and presently he dreaded the least contact with the world. He withdrew,—back to his family, and back to "being a child again,"—always with the fantasy of beginning life once more and of becoming a new-born man.

The patient suddenly interrupted the analysis about the time when memories of certain homosexual games with the younger brother were about to become revealed. He thought he was carrying a terrible thing on his soul. He felt he was able to return to his studies and that was well enough. My suggestion that it would be well for him to keep away from the family circle for a time he stubbornly resisted. But the nightly spells disappeared and he was able to sleep with the door to his room locked,—that much, at least, had been accomplished. But it was the last of his concessions. He trembled at the thought of having to stay away from his family. He turned to his studies with such eagerness and with such good results that his father thought he was completely cured and came to thank me in words overflowing with gratitude. The patient played at recovery, because he did not want to look more deeply into his inner self, he did not

want truly to know himself or to draw the ultimate
deductions that necessarily flow from such self-
knowledge. Three months later I heard that the
turn for the better was still lasting. He had no
further night spells and he passed his examinations.

I could quote numerous other illustrations to show
the influence of "spiritual advisers" upon their be-
lievers in the matter of the struggle against masturbation. I forego this temptation. A couple
of general observations are all I need add. I have
already referred to the stubborn fight of religion
against auto-erotism. The minister in the first case
recorded in this chapter very appropriately referred
to Romans 8.6: "For to be carnally minded is death;
but to be spiritually minded is life and peace."

That phrase contains the gist of the opposition
of religion to sexuality. It would be meaningless
if we did not know that death means loss of salvation, while under "life and joy" we are to understand
compensation in the other life. With admirable
persistence the Church has always insisted on the
sacrifice of sexual pleasure as the price of eternal
bliss.

The persistence of such a doctrine, transmuting
all natural values, would not have been possible
had the human race itself not strived to free itself
of all earthly trammels so as to attain a God-like
stature and dignity by overcoming the animal instincts. The auto-erotist exhibits in its most acute

form this struggle against and in behalf of himself. So long as he disposes autonomously of his pleasure sense, he thinks himself his own God. One of my patients who had gone through a severe struggle against the masturbation habit showed me his diary, which he began keeping during his twelfth year. After passing through a religious phase of abstinence he again began to masturbate, writing in large letters, on the first page of his diary, the proud word: *Autotheos*. It was the divine spark of Prometheus, the rebel, that flared up in this fighter's soul. Naturally the flame dies out almost as quickly as it flares up. The proud sense of self-sufficiency does not last. Our Autotheos, too, dwindled down to a pitiable neurotic, a being, half-free, half-pious, to the point of superstition, who finally sacrificed all his own precepts in favor of the great moral precepts of his religion.

It would be very interesting to use this case as an illustration showing how the repressed sexuality achieves its revenge by pervading the whole of the man's religiosity. That is the revenge exacted by every repressed erotism. It conquers the power that aims to repress it by turning it to its own uses. The case extensively recorded in the next chapter brings the proof of this fact very plainly before our eyes. *The repressed overpowers the repressing energy.* Thus, in the end man loses both his faith and his sexuality.

Our cases have shown us how important mental hygiene has become; specifically what a crying need there is for a reform of our principles of soul care in the light of the new psychology. Our teachers and our ministers must become familiar with sexuologic and analytic principles as well as with their application to education. Were we to examine the various writings of old fashioned ministers, and others, on the subject of masturbation, we would be amazed at the light manner in which they play with the health of the people. I quote, after *Pfister*,[3] from a popular brochure by *Hauri*[4] a Swiss minister of the gospel:

"When a young man does all sorts of things in secret, whereby he pollutes his body, his health suffers terrible consequences. He becomes dull and tired, his senses are weakened, he loses zest and will power. He grows weaker and weaker on account of the unholy temptation. His thoughts pursue him step by step, leading him again and again into sin. He loses the joy of effort. In appearance and behavior he becomes prematurely old; finally some disease which he might have otherwise easily resisted takes him before his time. How many a man has thus sunk into an early grave, while others have become miserable and sick, or depressed and weary of life!"

[3] *Loc. cit.*, p. 476 (of German edition).
[4] *Eine Konfirmandenstunde über das 7. Gebot.* St. Gallen, 1910.

Unfortunately there are many such Hauris. In order to appreciate the distance we have progressed within the last decade in this matter, I now quote the fitting reply which *O. Pfister*, another Swiss minister of the gospel, but one who practices his vocation in the light of the new psychology, has addressed to his colleague:

"Any one who has seen the plight of masturbators unable to withstand the fierce struggle against their sexual instinct, reflects with horror upon the evil consequences of such horrible warnings. *Hauri's* contentions are the more deplorable since the experience of educators and physicians has shown that such warnings fail by far to free the victims of the habit. Warnings against evil thoughts and unclean books, or against evil companionship, or against indulgence in idle dreaming, admonitions to be strong and resistant—that is about all *Hauri* has to offer—such obvious measures do not come anywhere near meeting the problem as it should be met. All who are unable to resist the enemy are threatened by *Hauri* with dire and deadly consequences and that in spite of the fact that according to the most experienced medical men, over 90% of our young men have indulged at one time or another in the habit. We have seen that very often a neurosis breaks out when the habit is suddenly cut off. And shall we turn with brutal threats upon our boys and girls? An ethically earnest educator should not permit himself to indulge in so unwise a course of action as *Hauri* has been led into through sheer ignorance."

Pfister then points out that masturbation is not to be fought with general formulæ, with uniform suggestions, or with talks about heaven and hell. He looks into each case applying psychoanalysis whenever he deems such a course necessary.

Following case illustrates the manner in which *Pfister*, as a modern spiritual adviser, goes about this task.[5]

CASE 21. A 16-year-old boy confesses to me that for about a year past he has been feeling depressed. His dreams disclose that he entertains death wishes against his parents. Only after some weeks he confesses his daily habit of masturbation, a practice ushered in by the stereotypic phantasy that a boy or, more seldom, his sister, is being spanked on the nates. He has had the habit for the past two years. For about that same length of time he has suffered from blushing and abdominal pains. The habit was cleared up through interesting the boy in climbing exercises during the gymnasium hour.[6] A few weeks later, during school recess, the boy pressed his limbs together under the

[5] *Pfister, loc. cit.,* p. 478.
[6] A very common occurrence.

seat in an effort to masturbate while witnessing a boy
being struck over the nates. Immediately the obsessive image began troubling him once more. Of
course the school episode reawakened earlier memories. Perhaps the earliest was the following painful occurrence dating back to the fifth, or possibly,
the fourth year: some one had scratched up the
wall in the entrance hall. A neighbor accused the
boy's sister of the deed. The boy immediately assumed the guilt, though not with the idea of shielding
the sister. As no other reason seemed obvious I surmised that the boy had given in to a masochistic
trend. Soon he regretted his unfair self-accusation.
The sister complains of the brother but is not believed; she is punished and while watching her being
struck on the buttocks, the brother, as he well remembers, had a sensation distinctly pleasurable,
although usually he witnessed such scenes without
any sexual feeling; sense of guilt also entered into
the situation. At one time he felt sexual excitation
when he himself was struck over the nates. In later
years the sadistic feeling arose only when the victim
of corporeal punishment was one of his colleagues
who had done him some wrong.

Thus the sadistic components became expressed
in conscious feelings only when hatred played a rôle.
On the other hand hatred enters in our case obviously
as repressed incestuous love. That is also the main-
spring that sets the obsession and the masturbation

habit into play. The pedanalytic reëducation proved a fairly easy task. As a pleasant compensation, in addition to the increased joy of work and zest in living, the boy's relations with the sister grew very agreeable, displacing the old quarrelsome attitude on his part.

Thus the minister's report. It is the path of future development that *Pfister* has so courageously adopted; the path that will lead the slaves of outworn ethical notions towards a new age. Instead of a threatening God, an understanding God, instead of external moral proscriptions an inner sense of right doing. Psychoanalysis holds forth the promise of yielding a new system of ethics.

This illustrative case of *Pfister's* shows that there is gradually growing a reform of our religious-ethical views, that sexuality is once more about to be accorded its rightful place in the scheme of things on the part of our forward-looking ministers. On the other hand we note also that certain analysts endeavor to exert their influence in the direction of a broader concept of ethical ideals on the part of their patients. I know that many analysts try to free their patients from the trammels of old fashioned ethical views and even preconize a religious or atheistic views. I do not consider this to be a desirable course to pursue with our patients, inasmuch as the neurotics' beliefs usually prove well grounded and such a course often may plunge the sufferers into new conflicts.   Our task is merely to make the subjects' inner conflict an open one so as to free the neurotics from their symptomatic sense of personal guilt.

Other practitioners go farther than that, preaching a new form of religion, thus themselves turning into preachers.

This has been most appropriately expressed by *Marcinowski* in his excellent book entitled, *Der Mut zu sich Selbst* (The Courage to Be Oneself).[7]

[7] *Marcinowski, Der Mut zu sich Selbst*, Verlag Otto Salle, Berlin, 1912.

Der Unterleib is der Grund dafür, dass der Mensch sich nicht so leicht für einen Gott hält.

NIETZSCHE.

VI

The Compulsive Mannerisms of a Philosopher who has overcome his Masturbation Habit—His Water-Closet Ceremonial—His Morning Ceremonial—Leaving the House—Mannerisms in the Public Park—Solution of his Compulsive Mannerisms—Psychology of Asceticism and Abstinence—The Craving for Intoxication—The Abstinence Movement a Social Phobia—Social Safeguards against Masturbation—Parents as Sexual Guardians over Children—The Asexualization of the Child—The Masturbator is His Own God—Fixation of the Habit through Contrariness (Negativism)—The Revolt against the Teleological Standpoint—The Schooling of Sacrifice and Love—May Masturbation be Uprooted?—Sublimation of the Sexual Energies.

VI

His physical body is the reason why man does not easily hold himself out as a god.

NIETZSCHE.

Any one who has the opportunity of analyzing a serious compulsion neurosis always has the chance of finding that all the symptoms of this trouble group themselves around masturbation. The following portion of a longer analysis I record in this connection because it illustrates the relations between masturbation and confession.

CASE 22. This is the case of a young man, 28 years of age, a student of philosophy, who remained backward in his studies, causing considerable worry to his family on account of his compulsory acts. In the first place he became so strict a vegetarian that he did not want to eat even milk, or eggs, because these are animal products. He lived on fruits and was physically so run down that his appearance was frightful. He complained of the most troublesome compulsive thoughts and compulsive acts. Thus, he suffered terribly from the fear of losing something. He continually kept counting his

249

possessions, such as those he carried in his pockets, to convince himself that he lost nothing. If he paid out any money, he had to count the change over and over, to convince himself that he had lost nothing by the transaction. That was but one of his numberless compulsions of thought and deed. The whole day, from morning till night, was filled with similar compulsive acts. Below I record a few of them, particularly the mannerisms on going to the water closet. I may state in advance that for the previous two years he no longer showed any sexual excitement. He had masturbated inordinately up till four years ago. Then he suffered from pollutions which troubled him as much as if he had indulged in the habit. But later on he became almost asexual. He would have been well satisfied with that state, but for the troublesome compulsive mannerisms that harassed him. These mannerisms embittered his life, turning it into "hell."[*]

We let the patient, who is a Russian, relate his trouble in his own way.

The bath-room ceremonial. While still in the room I feel my trouser pockets, although I can carry nothing in them, to make sure that they are empty. This I usually do in the following manner: I put both hands in my pockets at the same time and search. This I do in the following manner:

With the finger in the inner and lowest corner of
the pocket I start drawing my hand slowly out
so as to feel every bit of the inside of my pocket.
I feel or rather press with fair strength from time to
time the different spots that my hand passes over,
at the same time counting: 1, 2, 3, 4, 5, 6, and so
forth until I am through. The height of the number I reach varies. . . . Mostly I reach number 11,
but this is not a rule, sometimes I get through with
fewer counts. The second and third time I do not
examine so carefully; I do it with the fingers of
the whole hand and mostly reach number 4, in timing
my task. This I repeat several times. The right
pocket I examine often with the left hand feeling
on the outside, while with the right hand I am
searching within, so as to make the operation easier.
The examination of the hip pocket is more quickly
over as I never carry anything in it. I am usually
satisfied to touch it with my fingers on the outside
a couple of times, saying to myself: 'Absolutely
nothing in this pocket.' But often I feel impelled to
examine also that pocket more thoroughly, when I do
it while steadying it from the outside with my left
hand. This is done to aid the search but also as a
safeguard against inadvertently dropping something
on the floor when I withdraw the hand from the
pocket. That is also one reason why the right-hand
pocket I steady with the left hand, while I search
with the other hand.

Prepared with toilet paper, which I always keep in the same upper coat pocket, I go to the bathroom. I bolt the door and try it with care generally about five times; I always count: the last time I push with full force, in order to assure myself that the door is really closed. I look over into the yard with care to make sure that no one has seen me enter the bathroom. I remove my trousers so that they may not come into contact with the seat by any chance whatever. If the seat is lifted I put it down carefully holding a piece of paper in my hand to avoid direct contact with my hands. Then I jump upon the seat meanwhile looking around with fear lest someone should see me doing it. In this squatting position I attend to my needs holding with the left hand my garments, in dreadful anxiety all the time lest they touch anything about the place.

Before leaving the bathroom I examine first of all the seat in a very particular and thorough manner. First I examine anxiously the part of the seat next to the wall to make sure that I have not lost something or soiled the place, which under the circumstances is really not possible. That examination I carry out systematically by dividing the area of the seat with imaginary lines, generally in four parts and examine each part in order. Here, too, I count 1, 2, 3, 4, etc., and while counting the index finger of my right hand points to the corresponding spot, which makes the examination easier because there are really no separate areas. Each time I say: 'There is nothing here, nothing here.' I repeat this statement with every movement of the index finger, and each time I carry on the examination.

The examination of the fly-leaf part of the seat is the most difficult part of the ordeal. First I bend over to examine the rounded edge. I follow the circle with my eye point by point. At the same time I make corresponding round movements with my finger in the air repeating to myself: 'There is nothing here, nothing here, etc.' This part of the procedure takes very long, for I must repeat it several times. On spots where a possibility of soiling the wood really does exist the examination can hardly be searching enough. I must examine those spots over and over, timing myself all along, exactly as when I examine my trouser pockets. After that I turn my attention to the surface of the fly-leaf to see whether the flushing sprayed any particle of water on it. I must examine long and carefully to make sure there is no sign of soiling. After flushing I must go through the whole examination all over again. . . . I look over the seat, scrutinize the floor and the window before I leave.

On way to my room I look about fearing that some one will see me leave the bathroom. Once in my room I lock the door and try it to see that it is really closed. That I do by trying generally five times to force it open—then I examine the lock. Next I wash my hands very carefully and this I also do in a special manner. In Vienna I use a pair of old shoes which I put on when I go to the bathroom. These shoes have no sharp nails on their soles and I would never wear them on the street. Nor would I use my street shoes for going to the water closet because they may scratch the seat or soil it with street dust and leave a tell-tale mark that I use the seat for standing on it. Before going to the bathroom I put on these shoes, carefully tying the strings so that they would not touch anything. When I return I take them off and look them over with great anxiety to make sure that they have not become soiled,—doing this here also by my method of dividing into imaginary regions, examining each part separately, all the time saying to myself, while pointing with the finger, there is nothing here, nothing here, nothing here, etc.

The ceremonial on rising: First thing upon getting up I ask myself: how many hours have I slept? To estimate that I always glance at the clock when retiring; therefore I ask myself how long may have past before I fell asleep? I choose a later hour as the probable time—and count the hours to the time of waking up, then I deduct the time I have probably missed sleep through the night. That is not easy to determine. The minimum is seven hours. If I have arrived at this figure, I say to myself,

'Septem horas dormire satis est' the Romans hold,
and I am satisfied on this point. On rising I hang
the bedspread on the door so as to cover the key-hole
and make it impossible for any one to watch me
washing.

"The worst obsessions come upon me before leaving the room: all on account of a notion that I must
prevent losing something. I try the three drawers
of my dresser to make sure they are closed. I had
already locked them. The top drawer I try with
particular care because I found that it may be
opened even when locked. I try the hinges to see if
they hold and draw the handle towards me to find it
secure. This I do counting, sometimes to thirty or
more. The other two drawers I go through with
more easily. Then I try the clothes closet, going
through the same performance to find whether it is
closed. Next comes the sofa. I always take a few
steps off and examine it from a distance to see
whether there is anything left on it. I begin with
the pillow. There is a cover over it. First I look
over the left end edge of the pillow which is free of
the cover. Then I examine each edge in turn, in the
usual way, dividing the area with imaginary lines
and counting the places from above downwards.
Then the surface itself is gone over minutely in the
same way. It is divided in three portions by imaginary lines. The examination of the right edge is
soon over. Next follows examination of the sofa

proper, divided in three. The right division is quickly examined. Next I take under scrutiny the individual objects. The objects are always the same and must always be in the same order. As I fix my attention on each article in turn, I say to myself: 'Here is the flower vase—here the blotting paper— cards on it—some written—others blank. Nothing between the vase and the blotting paper.' Prolonged gazing (Doubt). 'Next. Here is the toothpaste wrapper (which I don't dare throw away), here is the lamp, here is the ink, the cup.' I look under the cup, under the blotting paper to see whether there is anything that escaped attention. Then I divide the table with imaginary lines into 3 or 4 parts and examine each part separately. While doing so I also try to take in each division as a whole. That I succeed in accomplishing after a certain time, requiring great concentration. Finally I draw with my finger in the air taking in the whole area under inspection as I say each section, 'Nothing here.' This I repeat with each section. Now I turn my attention to the dressing table. There is a cover on it. On the cover a cup, a water jug, and a glass. The examination of this cover is a tremendously laborious task. It had been folded so its folds divided it into four parts. I use that division in my scrutiny of it. I look for all other natural divisions or existing signs which would make my task a little easier. There is a certain conventional figure stamped on the cover. That figure enables me to partition off each area into smaller sub-divisions for more careful inspection. For the last scrutiny I place the water jug on the left side of the table near the wall. That is the first of my main four divisions of the table cover, the other three are measured by the eye. With each one of these I now proceed in my usual way, counting. The first of these gives me most trouble. It is the last about which I satisfy myself completely. The cup is on it. First I remove the cup and look under it. The cup replaced exactly in its spot, I search over the rest of the area which I further subdivide into very small spots for my purposes, drawing the imaginary lines from various angles. Finally as the result of considerable effort and concentration I succeed at a glance to take in the area as a whole. That is the most critical point in my ceremonial. A long time and considerable concentration are required. Again the four parts are looked over, this time each as a unit and more rapidly.

That done, I turn to the bed. I look to see whether I left anything under the pillows. Division in 3,—it is quickly over. Then the side table— again lingering. The candle holder is removed, the cover inspected carefully after the usual imaginary division into four parts. The holder is next inspected. There are usually two or three burnt matches on it. Each one of them arrests my attention for a while (doubt). Then I take off the table the piece of toilet paper I used the previous evening to wipe my fingers after applying a zinc ointment I use for eczema. I am always fearful that it may be a banknote and I examine it for a long time before I throw it into the slop jar.

Next I examine my pockets to make sure that my purse, watch and key are in order. Finally I stand for a while in the middle of the room and look around to make absolutely certain that everything is as it should be. This I do by pointing with my finger and repeating to myself: 'That is all right, that is all right!' There must be precise order and everything must be just so, otherwise I am compelled to start from the beginning and go all over again.

At last I leave the room, close the door after me very carefully and try the lock several times and touch the key repeatedly to prove to myself that it sticks. I go to the park, examine the bench I choose to occupy to see that it is not unclean and lay on it my coat, umbrella and hat. . . . I stroll on the path a few times back and forth. But before I can turn my attention to any serious work I must complete the examination of my pockets. I am now concerned whether I have with me the three objects, pocket-book, timepiece, key. This is a most distressing and lengthy ordeal. I begin with the keys. I carry them in the left coat pocket with mirror and toilet paper. I grasp the keys through the cloth from the outside

—the keys are bunched together—first one of them, and I say to myself: 'This key is here.' I take hold of the next key and repeat: 'That one is here' and 'the other one is here.' With that I press them as hard as I can to convince myself that it is so. Then I put my hand in my pocket to make the keys rattle. I turn to the pocketbook. It is in the upper left coat pocket. I put the hand in my pocket and let the pocketbook fall a few times to convince myself through the noise of its fall within the pocket of its presence there. Then I generally draw it out and press the pocketbook with all my force to make sure that it is closed. That I usually do five times, the last time slowly, deliberately and with greater keenness than ever. Then I look into my pocket to convince myself visually, first that it is there really and truly, and second, that it is closed. I gaze upon it for a long time in a very particular way by fixing my attention on each part of it successively. Then I let the pocketbook fall into my pocket again and again, while counting, and finally I feel of it from the outside a few times. With the watch I do likewise but more quickly. Then I go over the three objects again and again in a general way. In the Fall I wore a light overcoat for a time—then I carried the keys in the left, the pocketbook in the right trouser pocket. Now I often reassure myself by saying 'The keys were in the left pocket, they are in the coat pocket now, the pocketbook was in the right pocket, it is there, everything is all right. In the back trouser hip pocket I carry nothing.' (Searching.) 'Here are keys, pocketbook, watch'— every word I pronounce very distinctly—'3 things— the trinity is here—all's well.'

Other obsessions while in the park: If I sit down on a bench, I become uneasy, lest the seat be unclean. I turn around and examine it by my usual method of dividing with imaginary lines and timing myself while I turn my eyes from spot to spot. If I rise and walk trying to think of some problem, the thought of losing something comes to me in some such way as this: I happen to see a paper lying on the ground—I cannot make out what it is. I look at it, stamp upon it a few times, counting, or tear it with my heel. Then I pick up the paper and exam- ine every bit of it meanwhile counting, mostly to 5. After a little while another paper distracts my attention. I go through the same process with every piece of paper I meet on my way. Every little while I wonder whether the things I left on the bench are still there. If a man passes by I must stop and look around to make sure that he has not picked up any of my belongings. Or the thought strikes me that the wind may blow something away even though the air be quite still. Mostly I think of the coat and the hat—occasionally the umbrella also becomes the object of my anxiety. I return to the bench and say to myself as I point with my finger to each object in turn: 'The coat is here, the hat is here, the umbrella is here. Three things are here.' I prove it to myself in just this manner several times.

This uncertainty I also experience when I take the handkerchief out of my pocket. I inspect not only the spot on the ground where I happen to be at the time but every part of it up and down the whole length of my walk.

Leaving the bench is a very troublesome procedure. I am concerned not to leave anything behind. To reassure myself I examine the seat and the back in my usual way and the ground in front as well as under the bench. If another bench is nearby I look that over too, though more quickly. For that reason moving from one bench to another is very unpleasant to me as I have to go through the same procedure every time. I do not care to sit near other persons. Their presence disturbs me. I do not care to have them discover my troublous search so I must carry it on without outward aids, such as hand movements, and that makes it harder. I turn to the bench and fix it attentively in my mind as if lost in thought; and I do the same when I am in a store making a purchase and taking money out of my pocket. I am always concerned, lest I forget change on the counter, and I must reassure myself by my usual method of dividing and counting, but I carry that on unobtrusively and silently so the storekeeper does not know it. Furthermore, the notion strikes me that the overcoat pockets may contain something I do not know. I must investigate again. Often I am concerned with the pocket flaps. If they are stuck inside the pocket something may fall out and this thought makes me reassure myself by stroking each lapel in a very particular way while counting. If I put my hat and umbrella on a table, the thought troubles me that they may fall. I fix the umbrella attentively saying to myself: 'The umbrella is there, 1, 2, 3, 4, 5. It is in the middle of the table. It cannot fall. It is at least 20 centimeters from the edge from this side, also from this side.' I lower my head and eye the table closely so as to estimate the distance, and here, too, I have recourse to my imaginary division into areas and counting. So also when I sit at the table in my room I get the notion that one or another of the objects on it might fall and have to go through the ordeal of reassuring myself in the same way over and over. If I see a paper on the floor I have to pick it up, examine it at length while counting 1, 2, 3, 4, 5, etc. A burned match or cigarette stub makes me very uneasy. Somehow strongly bound up with my condition is my habit of spitting. I expectorate sometimes for hours at a stretch to get rid of my saliva. . . .

Among teetotalers I find a surprisingly large number of masturbators who abandon the habit only after tremendous struggles. They confess to me that usually small amounts of drink cause them to backslide and that abstinence from alcohol protects them against backsliding. This shows us the deeper motive of the anti-alcohol agitation which usually masks itself as a hygienic movement.

Many neurologists find the individual's behaviour with reference to indulgence in alcohol a symptom that permits significant conclusions. Those who are nervously unstable can indulge but little in alcohol and become easily intoxicated. In the case of such persons small amounts of alcohol are enough to bring to surface unwelcome instinctive trends. These facts admit no doubt. I shall record here but a few observations showing that tolerance for alcohol may be due as much to psychic motives as to a particular physical disposition. Alcoholic intoxication is a state precisely like sleep. *We sleep not only because we are tired but also because the unconscious is asserting its supremacy.* There exists similarly a will or craving for intoxication. Against this contention may be pointed out that certain neurotics drink excessively without becoming intoxicated. That naturally proves nothing more than the coexistence of a counter-will. This counter-will strives against intoxication, warning: "You must not lose consciousness. Otherwise . . ."

In our study of fetichism we shall become acquainted with the history of a man who has organized for himself a very complicated paraphilia, a wonder-

ful sort of fetichism. He feels continually the urge
of giving in to his cravings and to run after some
fetich, etc. In his despair he starts drinking so as to
rouse his courage. But after a few glasses a nausea
comes over him preventing him from keeping up his
drinking spree. As if some inner voice, a voice which
he does not perceive, were warning him: "Now you
have drunk enough, it is getting to be dangerous for
you!" If he attempts to keep it up he begins at once
to vomit. Here, as in many similar cases, we find
nausea serving as a protective wall against the instincts. It stands directly in the service of a moral
tendency, protecting the individual against himself.
At other times the subject drinks to excess without
becoming intoxicated. It means that his consciousness exerts sharp watch and permits him not to get
drunk.

A counter history to the above case is that of a
man who carries out his urolagnia always while under
the influence of small amounts of alcohol. But this
man carries out his paraphilia also without alcohol;
he even experiences intoxication without recourse to
drink. He is capable of going through intoxication-
like episodes without touching a drop of liquor. He
craves intoxication. In this instance alcohol serves
as an excuse. In the "morning after" state of moral
Katzenjammer he finds an excuse for himself in the
fact that he had been drinking. But his "morning-
after" *Katzenjammer* is at its worst when he carries

out some urolagnic act without having touched any drink. In that case the ready excuse is missing and he reproaches himself most bitterly. The leit-motiv of all neurotics, which I always take the opportunity of emphasizing, "pleasure without guilt" (*Lust ohne Schuld*), plainly shows itself in this behaviour. Of course, there are numerous variants to this motive and among them the restriction of the feeling of guilt plays a great rôle. In this instance alcohol serves as the scapegoat.

Viewed from this standpoint the movement for the suppression of alcohol discloses itself as a social phobia. Teetotalers do not drink because they are afraid of themselves and of their instinctive cravings. They protect themselves by transferring their fear unto the community at large. The neurotic, precisely, is the one who displays these two bipolar tendencies: displacement upon the extremely small or upon the extremely great (*Freud*).

Thus I have had under treatment a neurotic who liked to dwell upon the thought that in the course of the past thousands of years the vagina lost much of its perfection. The vagina of an Etruscan or of an Egyptian woman must have been an ideal no longer extant. This neurotic showed also a pronounced gerontophilia. But he transposed his unbearable conflict upon the historic realm. The unbidden thought about old women and decrepit females which often broke out plainly in his consciousness was turned into speculations about the Etruscan and Egyptian women. The aboriginal thought-formula, "the vagina of old women," and, specifically, "the vagina of an old woman," was enlarged and became the speculative thought about "the vagina among the ancients," a theme more easily tolerated in consciousness. We have here a shifting (from the intimately personal) to the extremely general. This process of shifting (from one extreme to another) is what transforms the father into divinity and broadens the personal conflicts into religious ones.

The anti-alcohol movement is likewise a shifting (from personal conflict) to the extremely general and up to the plane of a social problem, a subterfuge for overcoming more easily the subjective complexes. *Furthmüller,* in his highly suggestive work, *Ethik und Psychoanalyze* (Verlag Reinhardt, München, 1912) has shown that the neurotic adopts the proscriptions and inhibitions of the authorities as his commands. He does not obey external imperatives, he carries out his own will. He is master of himself. But in the case under consideration we note the reverse psychic process. The anti-alcohol propagandist transfers his own inhibitions unto a larger canvass, upon the whole community, so as to be the better able to stand them. He thus attempts to protect himself through public avowal, through flight into the public arena, *i.e.*, by raising to a universal compulsion the inhibition of which he personally stands in need. The well known thinker, *Otto Weininger*, has attempted similarly to protect himself against woman. His well known work, *Sex and Character*, was intended to build a wall between woman and himself so that he might preserve his chastity for all time. Perceiving that it was not possible to live in accordance with his publicly avowed principles, he preferred to die. . . .

Social movements undoubtedly have their origin in social causes. But it seems to me fairly certain that the individual is attracted to them through distinctly personal motives. I knew a physician who was a fiery apostle of sexual abstinence. He founded a provincial society with this aim and achieved great success with a speech having for its theme the fighting of sexual diseases through abstinence. This physician was functionally impotent and wholly helpless in the company of *puellæ publicæ*. What more natural for him than to hold the prostitute up to scorn as altogether beyond the pale! He thus shifted his personal intimate conflict upon the social plane. The aftermath of his speech is very comical. On the evening of the founding of the Society for the Fighting of Sexual Diseases he achieved with his speech against prostitution so colossal a success that he was stormily applauded and acclaimed. It suggested to him the secret thought: "this time you will perhaps succeed also . . . with the prostitute!" He now felt himself a whole man. No sooner thought of than done! After the meeting he went straight to a house of prostitution. A feeling of inferiority had made him impotent. The heightened self-consciousness made him again potent. After his successful sexual intercourse his views changed and he regarded the society as superfluous as well as ridiculous.

Let us draw the inferences which this statement of facts permits and apply them to our theme, masturbation. So many books are written on the subject and there are so many agitators who fight against the habit! May not these activities also be so many symptomatic acts of self-assurance, transpositions of the problem from the intimately individual sphere to the social plane? I have already stated repeatedly: everybody masturbates! Every one has had to go through a more or less troublesome fight to overcome the habit. A person needs to have his inhibitions fortified, he must surround himself with warnings and he wants to remind himself all the time: do not masturbate, the practice shortens life! Therefore the numerous books on the subject are but subjective outpourings, and never attempt to deal with objective facts. Moreover, we must bear in mind that the individual is governed by the social forces which surround him—whether he means to subject himself to them or not. The unfoldment of the race requires continually new and greater sacrifices. Man's duties become progressively greater, his participation in the pleasures of life, in the divine indulgences, become continually more restricted. Life must not be thought a picnic, a saraband of pleasurable hours. Life is precious when it is one of endeavor and work.

Thus we find that even physicians are thoroughly imbued with the tendency to asceticism and that they, too, are inclined to deny to man the freedom of disposing self-reliantly of his capacity for enjoyment. The physicians behave precisely as do the parents towards their children. Inasmuch as everybody masturbates, the physicians, too, must have masturbated at some time or other.

But all parents have also been masturbators in their youth. How does it happen that they rave so furiously against the habit? I know mothers who consider it the most serious task of education to protect the children against the masturbation habit. What consultant has not met during his office hours the distracted fathers who bring along some masturbating boy whom they want cured of the habit by force! Drugs are proscribed for the allaying of the "excited nerves," the children are carefully watched, they are swathed in phantastic and most ridiculous bandages, the father is in despair, the mother already sees her boy becoming feeble-minded or facing the fate of an inmate of some institution for the insane. Other fathers force the child to confess every morning whether he has indulged in the practice and treat the backsliding sinner to a horrible

preachment or even apply corporeal punishment,
thus turning into flagellants.

That is a revenge on the part of the fathers because they in turn had been robbed of the pleasure of
the indulgence. They now inveigh into the lives of
other children precisely as had been done unto them.
The remarkable amnesia of parents for their own
youth manifests itself particularly with regard to
sexual matters and it is in that connection that the
forgetfulness assumes most ridiculous forms. The
parents behave as if they themselves had led exem-
plary lives, worthy of a Cato, and usually know no
more shining example to hold forth before their
children than their own personality. The child is
forced to view with shudders the great abyss between
his own sinfulness and the angelic purity of his
educators. This cannot but lead the child to the
conclusion that he is wholly bad and sinful, as it did
the poor fellow whose compulsive thoughts I have
recorded above!

It is psychologically a very remarkable fact that
parents are inclined to deny to their children the
right to freedom in sexual matters, perhaps begrudge
them that right, and at the same time they try to
preserve for themselves their sexual prerogatives to
a very advanced age.

All parents want to delay the sexual awakening of
their children as long as possible. Mothers at the
sight of their sucklings already shudder when they

reflect that as grown-ups they will love "strangers" and be exposed to sexual dangers; I have found numberless fathers and mothers indulging in such thoughts. I knew once a remarkably beautiful boy. It was quite common to hear visitors say to the mother: "You must look out for that boy. All the women will run after him." The need of sexual protection was always emphasized. But parents are not the protectors of their children's sexuality, except inasmuch as they may warn the children against the seductive enticements of nurses and servants. However, at the proper time they must provide the right sort of instruction on the subject. That phase will be taken up in detail elsewhere, when considering the theme of prophylaxis. In the present connection I touch upon the theme only insofar as it concerns the subject under consideration. Parents always forget their own youth and have the tendency of postponing, as late as possible, the sexual awakening of their children, as I have already mentioned. I know a mother who said to me, when I advised her to permit her well-to-do, 24-year-old, son to marry: "I am afraid he will crumple at facing sexual intercourse. I cannot think of my child as a man, embracing a woman like other men."

Such an expression has also a deeper psychologic meaning. Parents do not want to permit their children the right to the free choice of pleasure seeking. They want to determine precisely when the

child shall experience gratification and when it shall
not. It was thus during early childhood and they
want that custom to continue. All pleasure and
gratification shall flow through parental grace. Subsequently the State assumes for itself the same right.
All laws serve to do away with the freedom of
pleasure seeking. Parents feel themselves their
children's God so long as they are able to act as the
arbiters in matters of pleasure and unpleasure.
After that they sink into the nothingness of their
human existence. They dominate the child, if need
be, with some conventional lie . . . but their dominion over sexuality they do not give up. They behave
like the Biblical Old Testament God. He, too,
threatens Adam: "But from the fruit of the tree of
knowledge of good and evil shalt thou not eat; for on
the day thou eatest thereof thou shalt die."

But Adam permitted himself to be seduced into the
knowledge of good and evil by eating of the fruit of
the tree.

"And the Lord God said, Behold, the man is become as one of us, to know good and evil: and now,
lest he put forth his hand, and take also of the tree
of life, and eat, and live forever," it was necessary to
drive the upstart from the Garden of Eden, and that
alone is the reason why the cherub drove him with
flaming sword out of paradise.

Is not this Creation account, the history of every
person? Do parents behave differently? They per-

plex the child's notions of good and evil and threaten him with the horrors of death. They drive the child out of the paradisaical state of indulging in gratification at will. They hinder him from becoming divine by tasting of the tree of life.

Masturbation and atheism present an intimate inner relationship. Every masturbator is *Autotheos*, recognizing no authority over his gratification-sense. But parents strive to remain the children's Gods. They do not care to show themselves as mere human beings. Therefore they forget or overlook their childhood punishments and the wayward child finds himself confronted with his holiness, the father, and her holiness, the mother, as unattainable exemplars. The tendency to deify parents is observable particularly under the form of mother-worship. On my part I think it most appropriate to love human beings with all their human shortcomings, allowing their frailties to be overshadowed by their virtues.

I have already referred to the parental tendency of sharing a portion of their children's libido, like handing them a bite of bread. We observe this repeatedly: Mothers are not jealous when the sons bring home a bride of their choice. Fathers, too, want to select their sons-in-law, and not a few predetermine a particular bride for their son; I even know of some, inconsiderate enough to take their sons to houses of prostitution. We find throughout a parental tendency to be their children's God furnishing them the opportunity for allerotic gratification. Therefore their opposition against masturbation is also carried on with particular bitterness. The practice of masturbation frees the subject from the social obligation of gratitude. The masturbator has himself only to thank for all derived pleasure. But the tendency is to make us thankful to some higher powers for all our gratifications. Thus it comes about that the masturbation practice becomes a sign of opposition to the parents. Children whose practice of masturbation is disregarded by the parents give up the habit without outside direction. The habit attains its strongest fixation whenever the child feels that it is doing something against parental will and he continues to indulge through neurotic stubbornness. I know many who as children always masturbated whenever their parents threatened to inflict some punishment.

I have stated at the outset that parents endeavor to bestow upon the child that purity which they themselves lacked at the corresponding period of their lives. That leads to deifying childhood. All the endeavours of humanity are directed towards approaching divinity, towards becoming God-like. Numerous cases of Christ-neuroses and Mary-neuroses (*i.e.*, identification with the Christ or the Mary type of personality) which I have had the opportunity of analyzing have convinced me of that.

Through their child the parents aim to achieve Divinity. The child noting that tendency strives to become human. The purer the parents want to preserve their child, the stronger become the child's animal propensities.

Thou shalt develop towards the outermost limits of humanity! . . . such is the imperative of culture.

This attainment of this ideal is the gist of your existence! exhorts the theologian. Your sexual instinct has meaning only when it subserves procreation! The gratification-sense is but an accidental concomitant to this duty! Love is not pleasure but a task! Not without reason does our age speak of "marital duties." Duty is compulsion, it implies the notion of purpose, it involves pre-determination.

Masturbation is a habit capable also of implying man's revolt against the principle of teleology, or purpose. Life's purpose and meaning are inherent in life itself. Persons asking themselves: What is the use of my living? are sexually ungratified. He whose life is happy and who is gratified has no occasion to question himself about the meaning of life. The meaning of life is a question solved for him through the very fact of his happiness. Unhappy persons are overcome by a sense of the hollowness of their existence and flee from life. But the rebellion against the notion of purposiveness in love may drive the individual also into homosexuality. In such a case the imperative of reproduction is not brought in between instinct and gratification: Love has no other purpose than the acquisition of pleasure.

But surveying man's struggle against masturbation, we find a tremendous mass of victims. Necessarily we find ourselves confronted with the question as to the deeper meaning of this struggle. Particularly since the agitation for the overcoming of the masturbation habit is a movement in the direction of the future growth and unfoldment of the human race.

The individual, too, goes through these struggles being impelled by social forces. All the capacity for love which was once directed upon one's self exclusively and was therefore coextensive with egoism, in the course of æons changed its character by becoming social. Man at first loved himself only, after the narcissistic and the auto-erotistic types of love (in the true sense of the term). These energies are still potent in man. It took a long period of evolution for man to learn to attach his capacity for love to his most immediate environmental objectives. Love thy neighbor as thyself! And may further growth not lead to a broader ideal: love thy neighbor more than self? . . .

Man's development may be reduced to the following fundamental formula: Man learns continually to love and give more. Looking back towards the darkest ages we have before our mental vision the type of primordial man, half animal, egoistic, thinking of himself only, and hating everything that stands in the way of his wish-fulfillments. Hundreds of millions of years passed before man learned to love. The schooling, and the outward sign of his developing capacity to love, was always "sacrifice."

The first divinities were feared. *Ehrfurcht* (*lit.*, homage through fear), the typical attitude towards one's divinity, is the rudiment of the primeval fear which was once universal. The first sacrifices were offered on account of the fear of the punishing, revengeful powers. Primitive man parted reluctantly with the gifts the altar claimed. He had not yet learned the highest form of sacrifice, the sacrifice through joy of giving. Even the Greeks, before whose cultural attainments centuries have bowed in admiration, offered their sacrifices only through fear and as a matter of expediency. In their hour of need the Homeric heroes remind their divinities of the past offerings. Zeus is reminded how many hecatombs had wafted their smoke to the skies in his honor, Pallas Athene is apostrophized as ungrateful when she leaves in the lurch the heroes who had offered her their rich sacrifices. Woe to the mariner traversing the seas who forgot Poseidon! Jealous and petty, the Greek god awaited his sacrifice and the heroes who forgot him he pursued with relentless revengefulness!

But the all-powerful seed of love was already

beginning to germinate in agreement with the spirit
of a newer age. The Greek loved his home with all
the fibers of his heart and sacrificed his life, if necessary, for its defence. The fatherland is the whole,
it is the social aspect of life in contrast to the individual life; it is a love larger than the individual life.
One dies for others only to feel that one is living for
one's self. But back of this sacrifice there still
hovered the idea of recompense in the life beyond.
In all religions sacrifice is for the sake of that other
life. Allah grants his faithful, who die for him, all
the earthly blessings, fourteen-fold; Wotan gathers
the fallen heroes in Walhalla for eternal combats
and immortal glory; Rhadamantis weighs the souls
crossing the Styx, separating the heroes from the
cowards. Even Christ, who requires the highest
sacrifice, promises as recompense life everlasting, the
deep immortality of the highest state of happiness.

Every religion requires sacrifice of the instincts
for the sake of spiritual values; it exchanges realities
for unreal values. Hunger and love, in particular,
form the background of religious delimitations.
Fasting and sexual abstinence are the theme of commandments; they are punishments; they are expatia-
tions as well as the means for overcoming the earthly
and for attaining divine-like states.

A number of clinical histories have shown us to
what uses this barter of eternal joy is being turned.
Masturbation is given up, sacrificed, for the sake of

higher gratification. The joys of asceticism over-
balance the pleasures of sexual indulgence.

But is this always merely an exchange in favor of
eternal bliss. May the choice not represent rather
the development towards a remote evolutionary
stage, a growth in the direction of an ideal which as
yet seems to us almost unattainable? The ideal of
sacrifice for the sheer joy of sacrifice? The stage of
a blissful giving-one's-self-away for the sheer joy of
yielding?

Masturbation represents man's aboriginal sexuality. Through it are expressed all the suppressed
and asocial components of sexuality as well as the
whole sexual nature of primordial man, who took his
gratifications wherever and whenever he felt inclined
to do so, totally disregarding any other considerations. The attainment of gratification was his most
important, his sole imperative. To-day man has
only his body for his own. He can still steal out of
it his gratification as in the age of the primordial
man.

It is plain that the higher our cultural ethical
requirements become and the more refined our love
life grows, the stronger must grow also the need for
masturbation. As the craving for self-indulgence in-
creases the more difficult it becomes to transfer one's
libido unto the environment. We can imagine a time
when masturbation must have played a very insignificant rôle. The primordial man knew no bounds

and took advantage of allerotic pleasures whenever opportunity presented itself. With the development of the ethical imperative "Thou shalt not!" the gratification of the libido had to be sought upon the auto-erotic path.

I believe therefore that the masturbation habit is bound to grow with the growth of culture. At the same time the reaction against this form of gratification must also increase. The struggle against masturbation becomes more fierce in the measure that the need of it becomes stronger. Every energy (or movement) carries within itself the germ of the reaction, or opposite energy. Pressure generates counter-pressure. The struggle against masturbation is at the same time the struggle against man's past; it represents the struggle against the anti-cultural primordial instincts of mankind. The "sacrifice of masturbation" is being more and more pressingly exacted from the individual.

We recognize the relevance of this struggle—in fact, everything that occurs has its justification, social movements representing the compromise of numerous determinants. Nevertheless, as physicians we must restore to each individual his sexual freedom and the possibility of getting well. We note that the human race has overdrawn the mark in its struggle against its own past, that thé necessary domestication of the wild primordial sexual trend has been prosecuted too harshly.

I feel myself also but a part of the great social wave which now unrelentlessly insists upon greater sexual freedom. But I indulge in no illusion, and I do not hold that we are witnessing the dawn of an unhampered, free sexual life. The unfoldment of the race proceeds in another direction demanding continually new restrictions upon our instincts. As physicians we witness with bleeding heart the victims of this terrible struggle and we must think of binding the wounds of those who fall. We are but Samaritans. May our work save ever so many individuals, —the struggle will not necessarily cease.

For so much of the loss of gratification as is exacted by the giving up of the auto-erotic trends, substitution must be devised. Without libido the individual perishes. The sexual energies are sublimated and transformed: in the appreciation of beauty, of nature, of art, in the pleasures of giving and in social activities man finds new sources of gratification. All the ascetic energies are not lost. Mankind turns them to its uses. Everything that is great and noble has its roots in the depths of sexuality. It is an old saying:

Οὐδένα γὰρ ἐνθουσιασῳὸν ἄνευ τῆς ἐρωτιχῆς επιπνολας
συϱβαίνει γίνεσθαι.

Mysteriously unknown forces operate within us leading us towards remote ends which we perceive but dimly. How intricate are the strands which

bind the past and the future together and weave us
into the fate of the Cosmos! How helplessly we
strive in the midst of life's stream, borne upon it
when we think we lead, driven when we think we
direct, tossed high and dry upon the land just when
we are about to boast of having reached at last the
unmistakable shore.

GLOSSARY

agoraphobia: a morbid fear of any open or public place.

ambivalence: the simultaneous existence of contrasting ideas, emotions, and reactions, such as love-hate, pleasure-pain. Used synonymously with *bipolarity.*

anuria: absence of excretion of urine.

aphasia: a loss of the power of forming or pronouncing words and the inability to comprehend spoken words.

arithmomania: an obsessive desire to count objects on every favorable occasion or to think persistently on numerical and other mathematical relations.

bipolarity: see ambivalence.

claustrophobia: a morbid fear of being in a closed or confined place.

coitus interruptus: sexual intercourse, interrupted before emission has taken place.

coprophilia: a tendency, characteristic of infancy, to be attracted by the excreta, especially the feces. In adult life, a paraphilia (see).

defloration: surrender of virginity.

enuresis: involuntary discharge of urine during sleep, bed-wetting.

erogenous zones: certain sensitive regions of the body where stimuli can induce sexual feelings and reactions.

exhibitionism: a morbid desire to display the sex organs. A form of paraphilia (see).

exopthalmus: abnormal protrusion of the eyeballs.

fetichism: a morbid erotic attraction to certain parts of the body or to certain articles of clothing worn by the object of attachment, usually resulting in sexual gratification.

flagellantism: the practice of whipping to arouse erotic excitement.

gerontophilia: a sexual attraction for elderly persons.

glossolalia: speaking in foreign or imaginary languages, occurring in religious ecstasy, psychopathic states, and hypnotic trances.

homosexuality: sexual attraction on the part of an individual towards individuals of the same sex.

incest: sexual intercourse between individuals so closely related by blood that marriage between them would be unlawful.

masochism: a paraphilia characterized by a morbid desire to be illtreated.

masturbation: the inducing of tumescence and orgasm by manual or other artificial means. Synonymous with *onanism* (see).

narcissism: the persistence of an early stage of psychosexual development in which the sexual object, or love-object, remains the self.

neurasthenia: a neurotic condition characterized by feelings of fatigue, worry, and lack of physical and mental alertness.

Oedipus complex: the unconscious desire of a son to possess his mother and feel hostile, or homicidal towards his father.

onanism: masturbation, auto-erotism.

orgasm: the peak of sexual excitement in coitus.

paralogy: psychosis (see).

paranoia: a psychosis (paralogy) characterized by delusions of reference, interference, and persecution.

parapathy: neurosis, disorder of emotions.

pedophilia: morbid attraction to children.

pedanalysis: the psychoanalysis of children.

psychogenesis: the origin and development of mental phenomena; the mental origin and development of peculiarities of behavior.

psychosis: mental diseases characterized by disturbance of intellect, delusions, and hallucinations.

repression: the mental process by which perceptions and ideas which would be painful to consciousness are forced into the unconscious while still remaining a dynamic force.

sadism: a morbid desire to illtreat the sexual partner, a form of paraphilia (see).

schizophrenia: a form of insanity where a split in personality is the most striking feature.

scotoma: a blind spot; a blind or partially blind area of the retina. *Mental scotoma:* inability to see a psychological factor in one's own neurosis.

trauma: an emotional shock which may cause a lasting disturance to mental functions.

urticaria: an inflammatory disease of the skin characterized by blotches, a burning or stinging sensation and intense itching.

voyeur: one who peeps at intimate scenes in order to obtain sexual gratification, a form of paraphilia (see).

INDEX

287

For Product Safety Concerns and Information please contact our EU
representative GPSR@taylorandfrancis.com
Taylor & Francis Verlag GmbH, Kaufingerstraße 24, 80331 München, Germany